D0941271

Famous Artists

With 177 reproductions,
including 44 in full color

A CHANTICLEER PRESS EDITION

Famous

Artists

of the Past

Alice Elizabeth Chase

Yale University Art Gallery

PLATT & MUNK, *Publishers*

NEW YORK

Published in 1964 by Platt & Munk, New York 10, N.Y.

*All rights reserved under International and Pan–American
Copyright Conventions. Except for brief quotations in reviews,
no part of this book may be reproduced without permission
in writing from the publishers. This book is published simul-
taneously in the United States and Great Britain. © SPADEM
1964 by French Reproduction Rights, Inc., all works of Degas,
Monet, Renoir, and Rodin.*

*Prepared and produced in collaboration with Chanticleer Press,
Inc., New York.*

Library of Congress Catalog Number: 64-10373

*Printed by Conzett and Huber of Zurich, Switzerland.
Bound in the United States of America.*

Contents

"I begin to show promise." The words were murmured by Pierre-Auguste Renoir on his deathbed. Like many great painters, he was his own most severe critic.

"From Success to Failure" might be the title of the story of the first forty years of Renoir's life. Born in Limoges, France, he grew up in Paris where his father, a tailor, eked out a bare living. At thirteen Pierre-Auguste was supporting himself by painting flowers on porcelain. A few years later he earned good pay decorating fans with figures like those used by court painters whose works he admired in the Louvre. Still in his teens, he had plenty of orders to paint the walls of cheap cafés with scenes from classic mythology. But the boy was not satisfied, and at nineteen, having saved enough to pay for a year's study, he entered a master's studio. The teaching was dull but gave him the training he needed, and his fellow students were alive with ideas. With one of them, Claude Monet, he formed a close friendship. Both loved color and were interested in discovering how to paint *light*.

The 1860's and 1870's in Paris were lean years for progressive artists. Monet and Renoir sold few paintings and often lacked money for materials. But they found that by laying bright colors on their canvases in broad strokes which would mingle when seen from a distance, they caught the effect of sunlight. The color, the rough surface of their paint, and the vague shapes of objects puzzled the critics. Soon these painters began to be called Impressionists, from their effort to capture fleeting "impressions."

Landscapes brought only small sums or did not sell at all, but fortunately Renoir liked to paint people, especially women and children. His portrait of the pretty wife and daughters of Georges Charpentier, a prominent publisher, was accepted for an important exhibition, the Salon of 1879. It was sufficiently admired in spite of its new style so that a few commissions for children's portraits followed. Renoir spent his money on travel—to Algiers, where, in the brilliant sunlight, he claimed he saw *white* for the first time; to Italy, Holland, England, Austria, and Spain. From the Old Masters whose works he studied in the museums he gained new inspiration.

Renoir's favorite models were his wife and sons, Pierre, Jean, and Claude (called "Coco"), and Gabrielle, who joined the family as nurse. At last his canvases began to sell. In 1900 he was made a member of the Legion of Honor. But he was suffering increasingly from arthritis,

PIERRE-AUGUSTE RENOIR

(1841–1919)

Exploring Light and Color

SELF-PORTRAIT

IN THE MEADOW

and by 1910 was confined to a wheel chair. He continued
to paint, his brush gripped between his stiffened fingers,
considering himself lucky to be able to move his arm.

Both Pierre and Jean were wounded in World War I,
and in 1915 Madame Renoir died. But in 1919 a portrait
was bought by the French national museum, the Louvre,
and the old man was wheeled triumphantly through the
galleries to see it. Late in the same year he died, conceding
that now, at last, his art approached success.

Pierre-Auguste Renoir

Women and Children

Renoir was among the young artists who met with Édouard Manet in the 1860's at the Café Guerbois in Paris. He was not much interested in theories, but he believed in Manet's principle that one must paint what one sees. He became first a Realist, then an Impressionist. He and Monet often painted the same view. But to interest Renoir it had to have people in it. To Monet, people were merely spots of color.

Lunch of the Boating Party at Bougival shows a group of Renoir's friends

MME. CHARPENTIER AND HER CHILDREN

LUNCH OF THE BOATING PARTY AT BOUGIVAL

DRAWING OF COCO

tier and Her Children, as well as the screen in the background and the fashionable bamboo furniture derive from the Japanese. *The Umbrellas* was probably inspired by a work of the great Japanese maker of prints, Hokusai.

Renoir's late method was described by a visitor to his studio. With thin pigment wet with turpentine he reinforced the charcoal sketch on white canvas, then reworked it with a thicker mixture of color, oil and turpentine. Finally the rounded figures emerged from "the colored fog." Painted in this fashion, the colors blending on the canvas, Renoir's later works glow with a pearly iridescence.

against a background of shimmering leaves and sun-flecked water. Light filters through the red-and-yellow striped canopy. The dishes, bottles and fruits on the white cloth sparkle and the people glow with a joyous love of living. Some can be identified—the girl with the dog became Renoir's wife, and Renoir himself appears, almost hidden, in profile at the right. Yet the painting is also an illustration of theories of light and color.

As time went on Renoir became less satisfied with Impressionism. A picture must do more than demonstrate a technical theory. He disliked painting outdoors in the brilliant sun. His early training and his visits to museums led him to seek permanent values of design and mass rather than the passing ones of sun and weather. Classic sculpture, the works of Velásquez and Goya, the color of the Venetians encouraged him to make his figures round and firm, though keeping the fresh color of Impressionism.

Like Manet and Degas, Renoir was influenced by Japanese prints. The diagonal composition of *Mme. Charpen-*

THE UMBRELLAS

For the eager young reformers fighting against the stupidity and corruption of the French government in the 1820's and 1830's, the caricatures of Honoré Daumier were a powerful voice. They sprang from his hatred of pretense and sham and an almost fanatic love of freedom. A cartoon ridiculing King Louis Philippe, however, cost the artist six months in prison. When released, forbidden to publish political satires, he turned his attention to the life and manners of the people of Paris.

Daumier was born in Marseilles, son of a poor glass-painter and amateur poet who moved the family to Paris hoping for recognition as a writer. Honoré at fourteen had already worked in a law court, and with a bookseller. His mother despaired of his ever settling on a trade, but Honoré insisted, "I want to draw."

Finally allowed to devote himself to art, Daumier copied classical sculptures in the national art museum of France, the Louvre, then the works of the great Dutch painters, Rembrandt and Hals, whose subject matter and boldness delighted him. A few months in art school gave him a grounding in anatomy. But most important for him was learning lithography, a new method of reproducing pictures. Drawings were first done with pen or crayon on a slab of fine-grained stone. When the stone was treated with acid and inked, thousands of impressions could be printed with it. The stone could be ground down and used again. In all, Daumier produced some four thousand lithographs commenting on the events of the day and poking fun at human nature.

Lithographs provided the steady income needed to support his parents, and later his wife's family, but Daumier longed for recognition as a painter. Artist and writer friends admired his paintings but the public, which delighted in his humorous lithographs, apparently cared little for these serious works.

In his later years Daumier's eyesight failed. He lived on a government pension in a cottage near Paris given him by an old friend. Belatedly offered a ribbon of the Legion of Honor of France, he refused. The year before his death a large exhibition of his work was held in Paris. Although it brought him little money, he took great satisfaction in the appreciation of his friends and favorable notices in the press.

HONORÉ DAUMIER

(1808–1879)

Spokesman for the Common Man

SELF-PORTRAIT

Humor and Pathos

Daumier had an extraordinary visual memory. He never carried a sketchbook with him, but wherever he went he observed. Back in his studio he opened his memory, as it were, and drew from it with astonishing swiftness, accuracy and vigor. On one occasion, engaged to paint a friend's portrait, he found the idea of working from a model so hampering to his creative impulses that he finished the painting from memory before the subject arrived for the first sitting. To assure a feeling for mass and volume he sometimes built up figures in clay. "That boy has something of Michelangelo under his skin," said his friend Balzac. The figures in some of his paintings have the massiveness of a Michelangelo carving; and *A Boy Running* is as real as sculpture.

Railroads became common in

THE MOUNTEBANKS

A BOY RUNNING

Daumier's day and provided subjects both comic and serious. Discomfort, irritation and boredom are caricatured in his lithograph of people waiting in the rain for a late train.

In both caricatures and paintings Daumier shows himself passionately interested in simple people and their daily activities. His lithographs point up abuses, human weaknesses, cruelties and stupidities with sympathy and kindly humor. His paintings are concerned with the sturdy endurance of ordinary people struggling for a living. Washerwomen with their children and heavy bundles move with dignity on the stairs to the riverbank where they do their wash. Street players perform stolidly for indifferent strollers or, with sagging shoulders, plod to another stand. Daumier's color, like his subjects, is dark: browns, blacks, grays, with occasional bright touches. Today he is ranked with the great draftsmen of the nineteenth century.

WASHERWOMEN

STREET SINGERS

TINTORETTO

(1518–1594)

Master of Action

SELF-PORTRAIT

Jacopo Robusti, called "Tintoretto," "the little dyer," was perhaps the first self-taught artist. His father, a Venetian silk dyer, had enrolled him in the workshop of the great Titian, but something about the boy seems to have offended Titian and he dismissed him after a few days.

To learn without a master was unheard of in the sixteenth century, but Tintoretto, only seventeen, set out doggedly to teach himself. He made friends with minor painters, helping with the decoration of furniture, door panels and walls until he had acquired skill in both fresco and oil. To master anatomy and foreshortening, he sketched Michelangelo's tomb figures from plaster casts which he brought from Florence and models of human figures which he posed in various attitudes. To study light and shade and their effect on color, he built little houses with sliding panels and experimented with natural and artificial light. He applied paint with broad thin strokes so that the canvas sometimes shows through, yet at a distance each energetic figure is convincingly constructed. His canvases are enormous. Once when asked how large a wall he wished for a painting he flung his arms wide, saying, "About three Tintorettos."

About 1557 Tintoretto married the daughter of a well-to-do nobleman. Their fine house, the Casa de' Mori, still stands. Contemporaries tell of musical evenings in the Tintoretto home, with Tintoretto himself playing the lute and the children taking part. Artists, musicians and people of note frequented the house, enjoying Tintoretto's graciousness, generosity and dry wit. Three of his eight children became painters. His daughter Marietta worked beside him wearing boy's clothing to enable her to climb about the scaffolds. His self-portrait, painted about the time of her death in 1590, shows him haggard and hollow-eyed.

At his own death in 1594, Tintoretto was buried in Santa Maria dell'Orto in Venice, for which he had painted several great canvases. In his will which entrusted everything to his wife, he expressed his own feeling for his profession when he urged his sons Domenico and Marco to continue in "so noble and honorable an occupation" as painting.

RESCUING THE BODY OF ST. MARK

were about to burn his body a storm broke. They fled in terror. Tintoretto sets the event in a plaza that suggests his own Venice, and his Christians are Venetian gentlemen; in fact, the one to the right of the camel is said to be Tintoretto himself. Their quiet dignity contrasts with the frenzy of the pagans. The composition opposes the mass of the foreground figures with the deep, empty space, their diagonal movement with the camel's rope and the driver on the pavement. A fallen man at the left clutches at a curtain the shape and angle of which echo the saint's body, emphasizing its limpness.

In another scene a Christian slave has been condemned by his pagan master for visiting the saint's shrine. In punishment his eyes are to be put out and his legs broken, but before the order can be executed the spikes and hammers miraculously splinter. Spectators strain and stare in wonder; the turbanned executioner swings around to show the broken hammer to his master. Only the

Saints and Heroes

Tintoretto's first important commission was a series of subjects from the legend of the patron of Venice, St. Mark, writer of the second Gospel. These were to decorate the great hall of the School (or Guild) of St. Mark.

One scene in the series shows Christians rescuing the saint's body after he was martyred. Infuriated by his preaching, says the legend, the pagans of Alexandria had killed him by dragging him through the streets. As they

STUDY OF A MAN ROWING

MIRACLE OF THE SLAVE

slave on the ground sees the saint
swooping down with arresting gesture.
The diagonal bodies of saint and slave
repeat and counter each other, the
saint's head thrusting inward, that of
the slave leaning toward the viewer.
The two figures are linked by a great
S-curve running from St. Mark's feet
through his arm to the executioner and
ending at the slave's head.

    Tintoretto's paintings resemble
scenes on a stage. Against a backdrop of
landscape or buildings, action is made
clear by a balancing of movements and
a handling of light that is as carefully
planned as a theatrical performance.

ST. MARTIN AND THE BEGGAR

THE
AN EYCKS

(About 1390–1441)

The World
Made Perfect

MADONNA AND CHILD WITH CHANCELLOR ROLIN

On the frame of a large altarpiece in a church in Ghent, Belgium, is a Latin inscription explaining that "The painter Hubert van Eyck, than whom none is greater, began this work which Jan, second in art, has completed for Joos Vijd who paid for it...." The date is 1432. It is generally assumed that Hubert and Jan were brothers, and that Hubert, the elder, died while the work was in progress.

Of Jan van Eyck more is known. In 1422 he was master painter for John of Bavaria at The Hague in the Netherlands. A few years later, now court painter to the Duke of Burgundy, he was sent to Portugal to paint a portrait of Princess Isabella, whom the Duke was seeking in marriage. The Duke stood godfather to one of Jan's children, twice presented the painter with six silver cups, and after Jan's death in 1441 gave a substantial sum of money to his widow.

ADORATION OF THE LAMB (See details on facing page.)

About 1430 Jan moved to Bruges, where he served both as a master painter for the town, ready to gild "six statues for the Town House," and as court artist. Records note visits to his workshop by both Burgomaster and Duke. When an economy-minded treasury wanted to cut Jan's salary the Duke protested, saying he "would never find a man equally to his liking or so outstanding in his art and science."

The *Madonna and Child with Chancellor Rolin* bears out this judgment. The painting of the spacious room, the portrait, and the distant view are far beyond the talents of other artists of the time. Most remarkable are the details—the garden with flowers and birds, the two people looking over the crenellated wall, and the sunlit town and winding river against the distant snow-capped mountains. Historians have tried without success to identify the city. It seems to be both an earthly city and a "City of God," fit for the Christ Child and His kneeling worshiper, the great Chancellor of Philip of Burgundy.

Jan van Eyck is the first Flemish artist to sign his works. He also adopted a personal motto of the kind usually reserved for the nobility, expressive of true humility: *ALS IXH XAN* (As well as I can).

Reverence for Man and Nature

The Ghent altarpiece is painted on wood with two doors, called wings, closing over a central panel. On the outside are portraits of the donors, Joos Vijd and his wife. Within, the central panel shows mankind gathering in paradise to worship the Lamb—Christ—upon the altar. From the corners of the earth come martyrs, gentiles in turbans, and Hebrew patriarchs and prophets. In the right foreground are apostles, priests, bishops and popes. Angels with censors, or bearing the cross, column, spear and sponge—object of Christ's passion—encircle the altar. From a richly carved fountain flows the Water of Life. Phrases from the Book of Revelation in the Bible come to mind: "And lo, in the midst... stood a Lamb as it had been slain.... And a great multitude... which no man could number, of all ages and kindreds, and people and tongues... stood... before the Lamb... with palms in their hands...." And they "fell before the throne... and worshiped God." All this takes place in a "new earth," fresh with flowers and fruits, that rises to a skyline with the towers and spires of "the holy city, the new Jerusalem." The dove of the Holy Spirit sheds golden rays, for "the

city had no need of the sun, neither of the moon... for the glory of God did lighten it...."

To the religious thinker of the Middle Ages, man and nature were the means through which the perfection of God could be understood. In van Eyck's paintings every flower and tree can be identified, the buildings are architecturally correct, the men are stout or gaunt, bearded or shaven, and these earthly forms have been given a quality that makes it possible to believe one is seeing heaven.

Vasari, the Italian historian who wrote *The Lives of the Painters* a century later, describes Jan as an "alchemist," the first to use oil in painting. Whatever his technical discoveries, Jan van Eyck by his "alchemy" made the world of man into an image of paradise.

FRANS HALS

(1580–1666)

The Love of Life

SELF-PORTRAIT

The prosperous burghers of seventeenth-century Holland wanted pictures of themselves, their families, and their homes. Thus the painting of portraits and household scenes became an important industry. Among portraitists, Frans Hals was one of the most sought-after and original.

Hals spent most of his life in Haarlem, then as now a small but prosperous city. His father, a clothmaker, had moved there from Belgium hoping vainly for a better living. Information about the son comes mostly from court records, for he was frequently in trouble. He had at least a dozen children (seven of whom became painters), and bills piled up. He was often behind in rent and even in payments for canvas and paint. On one occasion he was required to sell furniture to pay his baker. Yet he had a houseful of profitable pupils, and was paid well for portraits of military officers, clergymen, scholars and bankers. But money slipped through his fingers: he was a poor businessman, and he loved good living. Toward the end of his life, however, the town granted him an annual pension.

That Haarlem was proud of Frans Hals in spite of his debts is proved by praise in two histories published during his lifetime. His portraits were recognized as masterpieces. The distinguished agent of the States General stood godfather to one of his sons. The painters' guild made him an honorary member. The town appointed him official restorer of old paintings and he was buried with great honor in the Haarlem cathedral.

The handsome features of *The Laughing Cavalier* are painted carefully in contrast to the broad simple masses of his hat and collar. Lace cuffs and embroidered doublet show skill with detail, yet do not detract from the face. But the most striking characteristic of the portrait is the genial mood, the vivacity in the twinkling eye and the mouth with its hint of a smile. For all his personal hardships Hals reveals an unquenchable joy in living.

His self-portrait at about sixty, however, shows him tired, harassed and disheveled. The carefree gaiety with which he endowed so many sitters left him this time when he painted himself.

THE LAUGHING CAVALIER

Frans Hals

Merry People

With a mixture of detail and free, swift painting, Frans Hals portrayed the sturdy Dutch burghers and their wives. They look, as they obviously felt, secure and content. These are formal portraits, the subjects posed and serious in their fashionable grays and blacks.

It was when he painted his tavern companions and children

LAUGHING BOY WITH FLUTE

ROMMELPOT PLAYER

that Hals showed his greatest originality. These pictures, done for his own pleasure, seem to resound with laughter and well-being. They show us the ordinary people of Haarlem, the pose and expression of a moment caught with a few sure broad strokes.

A bright-eyed fisher girl, tub on head, pauses a moment, her face and hair damp with the sea breeze. A man with a kind of drum called a rommelpot laughs with the children who crowd around him to hear the funny rumblings made by rubbing straws on sheepskin stretched over a jar. The children may have been Hals' own. They appear again in the small round paintings, swiftly rendered, that show a grinning, toothless seven-year-old or a

LAUGHING CHILD WITH FLUTE

FISHER GIRL

chuckling youth with a flute.

Yet Hals could paint with precision and delicate finish. The detail of instrument and wineglass in *The Merry Lute Player* contrasts with the rough hair and carefree expression. The former are beautiful objects; the boy is a living being. The apparently casual composition is carefully balanced, the downward slant of the instrument countered by the youth's upward glance, the raised hand and glass played against the angled neck of the lute.

Even during Hals' own lifetime people began to buy these joyous paintings, and after his death they were so popular that many copies were made. Today they are among the most highly prized of his works.

THE MERRY LUTE PLAYER

25

HOKUSAI

(1760–1849)

An Old Man
Mad About Art

SELF-PORTRAIT

Painting in the Far East had been an art of philosophers and poets—men of culture and learning. With the same tools that were used for writing—brush and ink—a poem and the scene it inspired were painted on silk or paper. But in the seventeenth century a new class of artists appeared in Japan, painting new subjects called *ukiyo-e,* or "scenes from the passing world," which showed people in everyday activities. These were the means, in the form of cheap woodcut prints, by which Japanese art became known in Europe and America.

One of the most popular painters of daily life was Hokusai. Born in Edo (now Tokyo) in 1760, he was raised by a maker of metal mirrors. Later he worked with a bookseller and a wood engraver. At nineteen he entered the shop of Shunsho, an ukiyo-e painter, and learned to paint actors in the style of his master. This earned him the name of *Shunro,* for a Japanese artist or artisan may take a new name with each change in his position or his style of work. Hokusai in his long lifetime used forty or fifty different names.

Hokusai worked with driving energy. He was a good showman, once making a painting so big that people could see it only from the roofs, and another time painting two sparrows on one grain of rice. He wrote and illustrated novels, as well as a *Treatise on Coloring.* Some of his books are series of pictures: *Fifty-three Sights of the Eastern Capitol,* or *Views Along the Bank of the Sumida River.* In his seventies he turned to landscape and produced many views of Japan's sacred mountain, Fujiyama. In *The Breaking Wave Off Kanagawa,* snow-capped Mt. Fuji is low and distant behind the turbulent sea.

Hokusai married twice and had five children. His eldest son and grandson were wild and extravagant and kept Hokusai so constantly in debt that he had to hide from bill collectors, slipping into Tokyo at night to take paintings to his publisher. With his youngest daughter, Oei, herself a painter, he lived cheaply, moving often—as many as ninety-three times—to escape accumulating dirt and back rent. Yet he was proud, and when a great actor, in disgust at the dirty floor, spread a cloth to sit on, Hokusai was so offended that he refused to deal with him, much as he needed his patronage. When he was seventy-eight his house burned, destroying all his notes and drawings. But he continued to paint to the very day of his death, and left at least thirty thousand pictures.

"Random Sketches"

Although many of Hokusai's paintings survive, his work is best known to us through woodcuts made from his designs. To produce them a craftsman copied the original drawing on a wooden plank and gouged away all parts that were to be white in the finished print. The process is similar to that used by the sixteenth-century German, Albrecht Dürer, but the Japanese artist added color, at first by hand, and later by cutting a separate block for each color and printing one on top of the other. Sometimes as many as twelve blocks were used for one picture. Hokusai

HARVESTING

PEOPLE IN RAIN

SWIMMERS

27

NOBLES PRACTICING HORSEMANSHIP

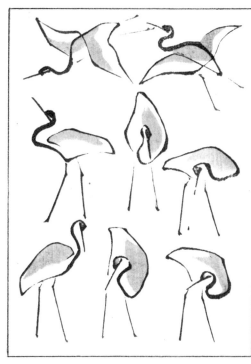

CRANE (See detail on facing page.)

knew how to cut blocks and could thus direct the men working on his designs.

In 1814 Hokusai published a small book, the first of fifteen volumes, which he called his *Manga,* or *Random Sketches.* Three wood blocks were used for each plate—gray, pink, and black. The *Manga* gathers together an amazing variety of drawings. Men and women, nobles and laborers, animals, birds, insects, reptiles, plants, flowers, trees, figures of saints and devils, buildings and machines cover one page after another. They are the daily notes of a keen observer of the world and bring to us delightful glimpses of the many-sided life of Japan. One enjoys the pattern of umbrellas on a rainy day, or the spirited horsemanship of nobles. One sees swimmers, rice harvesters in the field, and bargemen on their boats. All reflect the delight in the "passing world" which is the essence of *ukiyo-e.* Sometimes in the use of vanishing-point perspective Hokusai reveals the influence of European art which

BARGES

he saw in books or prints or even a few paintings brought into Japan; but he deplored the fact that "in the European method they attempt to... deceive our eyes."

At seventy-five, Hokusai wrote, "From the age of six I had a mania for drawing.... At seventy-three I learned a little about the real structure of nature.... When I am eighty I shall have made still more progress; at ninety I shall penetrate the mystery of things.... When I am a hundred and ten everything I do... will be alive." He signed it with the last of his many names: "An Old Man Mad About Art." On his deathbed at eighty-nine, he said to Oei, "If heaven would only grant me ten more years... I would have become a real painter."

HOLLOW OF THE DEEP-SEA WAVE

EL GRECO

(About 1545–1614)

Visions of

Heaven and Earth

Tall, gaunt saints of glittering mosaic adorn the walls of the monasteries and churches of Crete, that Greek island-crossroad of the Mediterranean. Their long, flat bodies and wide, staring eyes are unnatural but intensely expressive. Thus a love of rich colors and textures and a disregard for accuracy in painting man came naturally to Cretan-born Domenikos Theotoko-poulos, called El Greco, or the Greek. For several centuries the island had been under Venetian control, but in the 1560's the Turks were harrying its coasts. This may have caused El Greco in his mid-twenties to seek the greater security of Venice.

A few years later, in 1570, a Roman miniaturist wrote to a friend about a young Cretan, who had recently arrived in Rome, "a pupil of Titian, who seems, in my opinion, to have a rare gift for painting." This reference, a few signed paintings, and the obvious influence of the great Venetians, as well as of the older masters, Raphael and Michelangelo, tell us all we know of El Greco's Italian sojourn.

By 1577 he was in Spain, settled in Toledo. If he came hoping to share in the decoration of the Escorial, the palace-monastery-tomb being built for Philip II, he was disappointed. Neither of the two pictures he painted for the king pleased Philip, and El Greco remained in Toledo, working for its aristo-crats and churchmen.

Spain under Philip II was seething with a religious fervor that was expressed by the fanatic excesses of the Inquisition, the mystic visions of St. Theresa, and the discipline of St. Ignatius Loyola. This spiritual climate was congenial to El Greco. Apart from portraits, his subject matter was almost entirely religious. In such works, where spiritual content was of first importance, he elongated bodies, distorted gestures, and used a flickering, restless light to lift the event out of the world of physical reality. Even in the *View of Toledo,* one of his rare landscapes, which shows the walls, palace and cathedral of the city on its barren mountain, storm clouds lower with the menace of Judgment, and the buildings glow with an unearthly incandescence.

A painting by El Greco which is thought to be a self-por-trait reflects a haunting torment, explained perhaps by the contradictions of his life. He and his "trusted Jeronima" paid enormous rent for twenty-four rooms in a beautiful but dilapi-dated palace, but the furniture he possessed at his death would hardly have sufficed for two rooms. His library was large and scholarly; musicians were hired to play during meals; among his friends were high officials of church and state, yet his per-

PRESUMED SELF-PORTRAIT

sonal belongings included but one good suit. He and his assist-
ants, among them his beloved son, Jorge Manuel, were loaded
with commissions, but court records testify to scanty funds, to
debts owed, and to lawsuits for money due.

Pacheco, Inspector of Paintings for the Inquisition, preparing to write his book, *The Art of Painting*, visited El Greco in
1611. A conservative, he was puzzled by the old man's theories,
yet he concluded: "... we cannot exclude him from the ranks of
the great painters when we see certain things from his hand so
lively and vigorous ... that they match those of the greatest men."

BURIAL OF THE COUNT OF ORGAZ (See details on facing page.)

Men and Saints

In 1586 El Greco accepted a commission for an altarpiece sixteen feet high and twelve feet wide for the Church of St. Thomas in Toledo. The *Burial of the Count of Orgaz* was the result. Early in the fourteenth century, the count, wishing to be buried in the church, made large gifts for its reconstruction. He also ordered an annual gift for the poor of the parish of seventeen chickens, wine, firewood and cattle. At the count's death in 1312, said the legend, two saints descended from heaven to lay him in his grave. Fifteen noblemen of Toledo witnessed the miracle. Two hundred years later the parish ordered a painting in memory of the occasion.

El Greco divided the scene into an earthly and a heavenly sphere. Below, framed by a hooded monk and a priest reading the service, and backed by a frieze of spectators, the miracle takes place. The young deacon, St. Steven, and the aged bishop, St. Augustine, both richly clothed, tenderly lower the count's body, sheathed in polished steel armor. His pale face matches in nobility those of the attendant grandees. Costumes and portraits belong to the Toledo of El Greco's time. The face directly above St. Steven may be a portrait of El Greco himself. The kneeling boy looking at the spectator and pointing to the miracle is probably eight-year-old Jorge Manuel. The detail of the vestments, the embroidery, the lace of the ruffs, are worthy of a miniaturist.

El Greco

Above, heaven opens in glory to receive the angel who, with wing and drapery slanting earthward, bears up the soul of the count. The light of earth becomes, above, charged with lightning. The quiet mood turns to quivering ecstasy as John the Baptist kneels, appealing to the Virgin to intercede with Christ for the count's soul. St. Peter with his keys, and St. Thomas, patron of the church, identified by a carpenter's square, sit on either side. The slender, ethereal Christ seems to glow with inner light.

The presence in one canvas of naturalistic portraits and of distorted, elongated figures in unearthly light, refutes the claim that El Greco had defective eyesight or painted as he did because of madness. His exaggerations for the sake of spiritual expression anticipate those of modern painters.

VIEW OF TOLEDO

Most famous of the so-called "primitive" painters, Henri Rousseau was slow to develop, trying first one thing, then another. In school he enjoyed poetry and music, and liked to draw. He studied violin for a time, and learned to play the clarinet. Perhaps in search of adventure, he served in the army. Later his father, a tinsmith, took him into his shop, but Rousseau became restless and moved to Paris. There he married Clémence Boitars, the daughter of a furniture dealer.

Through Clémence, Rousseau secured an appointment as custom's officer at one of the gates of Paris, and from this position, which allowed him to retire at forty with a small pension, he got the nickname of *Douanier*, or Customs Officer, by which he is often identified.

Rousseau was almost forty when, encouraged by his wife, he began to paint, teaching himself by copying paintings in the Louvre Museum in Paris and by getting occasional criticisms from an established artist. His life followed a simple routine. He spent the mornings painting, the afternoons teaching singing and violin to the children of the shopkeepers of his district. Then he would walk to the Botanical Gardens where he was admitted after hours by a sympathetic attendant. At home in the evening he would paint again, then write poems and plays.

The musical evenings he arranged for his pupils became famous. The audience was mostly of uncritical parents, but gradually intellectuals began to attend, partly to laugh, partly out of appreciation of his simple honesty. He became acquainted with the group of progressive artists called "the *Fauves*," who allowed him to exhibit with them in 1905. Picasso, later to become world-famous, bought one of his paintings, and arranged a party in his studio honoring the old man.

Rousseau's last years were shadowed by an unfortunate love affair. Finally, "because his blood was turned to worry," as he told a friend, he inflicted a wound on his leg which became infected and caused his death.

HENRI ROUSSEAU

(1844–1910)

Haunting Dreams

SELF-PORTRAIT

Henri Rousseau

The Familiar and the Exoti

The paintings of Henri Rousseau were produced by a self-trained artist who admired realism but confused reality with dreams. Rousseau was a naïve workingman who believed in himself as an artist and had a genius for color and design. He painted with a direct, childlike vision unaffected by scientific theories.

A large proportion of Rousseau's work consists of views of Paris or nearby towns, vases of flowers, and portraits of his friends. In spite of his realistic intent he occasionally altered buildings, adding a lamp post here or cutting something out there, probably hardly conscious of these changes resulting from his natural sense of design. For portraits, knowing nothing of anatomy, he used a tape measure on his model to find the length of the nose or the distance between the eyes. Flowers he flattened into a tapestry-like pattern. Often he supplemented observation and memory by working from photographs or postcards.

Rousseau believed literally in ghosts and magic. He once told a friend that he could not stop painting because his dead wife was moving his hand and brush. In the Botanical Gardens, while sketching exotic plants and flowers with meticulous accuracy, he breathed the moist, hot air laden with strange odors. Later in his studio, painting one of his magical scenes of tropical forests, he would throw open his windows, feeling himself smothered by the smell of imaginary flowers.

His method was that of the self-

TIGER IN THE RAIN

RABBIT EATING A CARROT

taught artist. Over a preliminary sketch on the white canvas he worked inch by inch, finishing as he went, never retouching. A biographer has discovered that he confined himself to twelve pigments, working out his design with a balance of warm and cool colors. His jungles are rich mosaics in paint, yet he liked a work to be well-finished and smooth. He combined two worlds, the one he saw around him and the one that existed in his dreams, giving the streets of Paris a magic stillness, and the jungles the order of well-kept parks.

ROAD IN THE SUBURBS

EXOTIC LANDSCAPE

Monet ... Manet (see Page 50). That two men with such similar names lived in Paris at the same time, were artists with similar ideas, and became friends, is a series of coincidences that has caused confusion ever since. When Manet saw two landscapes signed "Monet" he thought someone was playing a trick on him. Convinced by a friend that there was such an artist, and realizing that his work was good, he welcomed Monet to the discussions at the Café Guerbois.

As a boy in Le Havre, Monet was a successful caricaturist, but a friendship with Boudin, a local realistic artist, introduced him to an ideal which became his passion: to learn to see, and to paint what he saw. Academic artists usually studied the art of the past and painted things as they thought they looked rather than as they actually saw them. Sent to study in Paris, Monet revolted against this academic method. Experiment, discussion, and above all, *looking,* led Monet to paint landscapes sparkling with sun and air. But his paintings with their bright colors and rough surfaces did not sell at first and he endured years of hardship. He was often even hungry, living on the bread which his friend Renoir brought stuffed in his pockets, or on leftovers from a restaurant where they painted. To save rent he built a studio-boat where he and his wife and son lived while he painted sunlight and mists on water and riverbank. Friends came to paint with him— Renoir and others, and eventually even Manet.

In 1874 a group of these artists arranged an exhibition in Paris. The title of one of Monet's paintings, *An Impression: Sunrise,* was seized upon by critics who mockingly called the group Impressionists. Few paintings sold, and for Monet hardship became tragedy when, after the birth of a second son, his wife died.

But in England during the war of 1871 Monet had met a young and enthusiastic art dealer who bought an occasional canvas. In the mid-1880's his paintings began to find a market, first in America, then in Europe. By 1890 the years of poverty were over. Monet bought a house at Giverny, twenty miles from

CLAUDE MONET

(1840–1926)

"An eye, but what an eye!"

PORTRAIT OF CLAUDE MONET, BY THEODORE ROBINSON

Paris, where he diverted a stream to make a pool, built an arched Japanese bridge, and planted willows, water lilies and exotic flowers. During the rest of his life this garden was the subject of most of his paintings.

In 1917 Monet began wearing heavy glasses. Six years later, nearly blind, he underwent an operation which restored the sight of one eye. Then he himself had the experience he claimed he tried to render in the blazing color of his late canvases—that of a blind man who suddenly sees.

AN IMPRESSION: SUNRISE

Claude Monet

TWO HAYSTACKS

JAPANESE FOOTBRIDGE AND LILY POOL

WATER LILIES (Detail)

Dissolved in Light

To paint what you see, as the Impressionists tried to do, sounds easy, but few of us really use our eyes. Monet (to quote his friend Cézanne) "had the most prodigious eye since there have been painters." As he analyzed what he saw, he came to the conclusion that since we see nothing in absolute dark, what we see is light reflected from objects. Light, he found, is not merely white or yellow, but rich with color. If you mix colors on your palette the results are muddy and dull, but if you put them side by side and stand back from the canvas, they blend in your eyes and make a livelier effect. So Monet covered his canvases with daubs or dots of color which become recognizable objects only when seen from a distance. He could paint as precisely as any realist, but to capture the effects of light and atmosphere he sacrificed mass, weight and detail. People became mere blobs of color.

From Boudin, Monet learned to notice how colors change if the sun goes under a cloud, if the air is misty, or the wind rises. Boudin would date each sketch, noting the time of day, the weather, and even the direction of the wind. If he wanted to do more work on a sketch he would wait for a similar day.

Monet was one of the first to paint landscapes entirely out of doors. Realizing that he was painting light, and that light changes every moment, he made series of pictures of haystacks or poplar trees at different seasons and different times of day. From a window opposite Rouen Cathedral he made a dozen or more paintings between dawn and evening, each recording as exactly as possible the light on the façade during one brief period. He is said to have had at least a hundred canvases of the Thames River in London under way at the same time.

The sky, water, reflections, trees and flowers of the garden at Giverny offered infinite variations, infinite challenge. During the thirty years he painted there, his color grew more and more brilliant. Objects still show vaguely, but color suggests more than how they look. It glows with the artist's fiery enthusiasm, his deep love for the garden which was his delight for so many years.

Monet's way of seeing and of painting had enormous influence on his contemporaries and successors, and his late works even foreshadow those of the so-called Abstract Expressionists of the mid-twentieth century.

ADIOLAS

Eugène Delacroix was born near Paris in 1798, that period after the Revolution when France was stirring with pride over the victories of the young Napoleon. Something of the excitement of the times seems to have entered the child; his artistic career was to be a revolt against the rigid drawing and dull color of classic taste, and a plea for vigor, vitality and freedom in art.

In his school days Delacroix showed talent on the violin, and throughout his life he was strongly influenced by music and musicians. One of his intimate friends was the composer, Chopin. But he also loved to draw, and when a disastrous lawsuit left his family destitute, he chose painting for his career.

Delacroix's teacher in the School of Fine Arts in Paris was a classicist interested in precise linear outline and quiet color, but many of the young painter's friends were romantics, as enthusiastic as he for rugged, expressive drawing and rich, vibrant color. On a visit to England in 1825 he learned a great deal from the English colorists. For subject matter he turned to medieval history and to literature: the plays of Shakespeare, the works of Scott, Byron and Goethe. A masterpiece shows *The Crusaders Entering Constantinople*. Dark figures with fluttering banners loom against a background aglow with flame. The disorder of war is made comprehensible by this vivid and dramatic composition.

In 1832 Delacroix was invited to accompany a special mission to the Sultan of Morocco—the first artist to visit what was then a remote and wild country. For six months he traveled about Morocco and Algiers, with a brief interlude in Spain, filling notebooks with sketches, descriptions and comments. The mission returned to France loaded with gifts which included horses, a tiger, a lioness, ostriches, gazelles and a pair of antelope. Many aspects of this experience were reflected in his later paintings.

Throughout his career Delacroix's paintings suffered abusive criticism, yet many of his works were bought by the state and he received government commissions to decorate some of the most important public buildings in Paris. From time to time he won medals

EUGÈNE DELACROIX

(1799–1863)

Fear and Fury

SELF-PORTRAIT

at the annual Salon, and he was made a member and finally an officer of France's Legion of Honor.

Delacroix was strikingly handsome, and as a young man was something of a dandy, fond of fencing, horse-back riding, and fashionable parties. But for many years he suffered from recurring periods of fever. Eventually he became almost a recluse, devoting all his energies to his work. Although his illness grew worse he was de-scribed by a friend a few years before his death as look-ing "as proud, as sharp... as a tiger."

THE CRUSADERS ENTERING CONSTANTINOPLE

COMBAT BETWEEN AN INFIDEL AND A PASHA

COMBAT OF A LION AND A MAN

Battles of Men and Beasts

Delacroix was the leading romantic painter of the nineteenth century. In compositions of violent action he expressed the intensity of such emotions as courage and terror, love and hate. His huge *Journal* sets forth his theories: To tell the truth one often must exaggerate. The expression of a figure comes through "furious movement and flowing gesture." "A hand should speak like face," he writes. The most important means of expression, he asserts, is *color*. From the English he had learned the value of laying strokes of bright color side by side. "The more contrast, the more brilliance." Under the blazing sun of North Africa he saw that shadows are not black but contain the complementary color: a red face shades into green, a yellow wall turns purple. His color discoveries were later of great interest to the Impressionists.

Like Daumier and Goya, Delacroix was obsessed with the idea of struggle— man against man, man against beast, beast against beast. Daumier showed the common people struggling with poverty and oppression; Goya painted the struggle in war and in the bull ring of his own Spain. But in Delacroix's scenes costumes and weapons belong to the remote world of Africa and the East, or the imaginary one of popular romances. Turk and infidel meet in combat made breath-taking by the note of treachery as well as by the violent diagonals of spirited horses, flowing garments, and slashing weapons.

AN ARAB CAVALIER

THE LION HUNT

Delacroix studied and sketched animals in the Paris zoo, even securing permission to dissect any that died. Lions and tigers fascinated him. He drew them attacking other animals and even men. In *The Lion Hunt,* beasts, horses and men writhe in combat, the shadowed landscape and stormy sky adding to the sense of violence.

In spite of poor health, Delacroix accomplished an astonishing amount of work. Almost a thousand paintings, some fifteen hundred watercolors and pastels, and more than six thousand drawings testify that he shared the energy he depicted.

J. M. W. TURNER

(1775–1851)

Poet in Paint

PORTRAIT OF TURNER, BY J.T. SMITH

"I have met with a good-tempered, fussy, little elderly gentleman.... He is continually popping his head out of the window to sketch whatever strikes his fancy.... The name on his trunk is... J. M.W. Turner." Thus a fellow traveler crossing the Alps in 1829 described the great English painter whose innovations in oil and watercolor helped to revolutionize the painting of landscape.

James Mallord William Turner was born in London in 1775, the son of a barber who boasted, "My son is going to be a painter." His boyhood sketches, displayed around the shop, sold for a few pennies each. At fourteen, he was accepted as a student in the Royal Academy, where he received a thorough technical training; but it was from the French, Dutch, and Italian landscapists of the seventeenth and eighteenth centuries that he learned to relate foreground and distance and to suggest air and space.

Throughout his life Turner made a steady income from sketches in pen and watercolor of the country estates of English gentry. The paintings were based on studies made on the spot, and at first followed the old conventions—dark foreground against light distance, and a color scheme of subdued greens and browns. But as he traveled about England, Scotland, and Wales, he realized the limitations of this rigid system. His color schemes grew lighter and brighter in an effort to do justice to the brilliance of sunlight.

Perhaps no artist has ever traveled and sketched so much. He visited Europe many times, delighting in Rhine castles, Alpine heights, and Roman ruins. Venice enchanted him with its warm color and changing weather effects. He loved the sea and knew ships well, sailing along the coast in fishing smacks and in coal-bearing freighters.

Turner's works were severely criticized by older conservative artists. His paintings are "crude blotches, nothing could be more vicious," said Benjamin West, President of the Royal Academy. But from the beginning they won the approval of the more progressive artists and the general public. He was elected to the

GRAND CANAL, VENICE

Royal Academy at twenty-seven and later appointed
Professor of Perspective. His pictures sold well, and
being a shrewd businessman, he accumulated a large
fortune. He never married, but his father lived with
him and managed the household. As he grew older,
Turner became more eccentric, living under the name
of "Mr. Booth." At his death in 1851 he was buried in
the crypt of St. Paul's Cathedral beside England's greatest artists. His will included a bequest to the British
nation of two hundred and eighty-two paintings and
a staggering total of almost twenty thousand drawings
and watercolors.

Sunlight and Storm

THE SLAVE SHIP

Although a realist in his insistence on accuracy, Turner was a romantic who saw the world with the eye of a poet. He loved to paint dawn and sunset, mist, cloud and storm. Heights crowned with ruined castles and ravines spanned by picturesque bridges delighted him. He became obsessed with the desire to paint light and air and he experimented with techniques to accomplish it.

In watercolor the white paper, shining through layers of transparent pigment, lends brilliance to the colors. Realizing this, Turner used this medium, which had commonly served only for quick sketches, for finished works. He captured similar freshness in oil by priming the canvas with white instead of the usual dark ground. His handling of color, which was described by a contemporary as painting "trees blue and yellow" to "produce the effect of green at a distance," anticipates Impressionism by fifty years. So does his use of coarse canvas to break up his brush strokes.

THE SHIPWRECK

ULYSSES DERIDING POLYPHEMUS

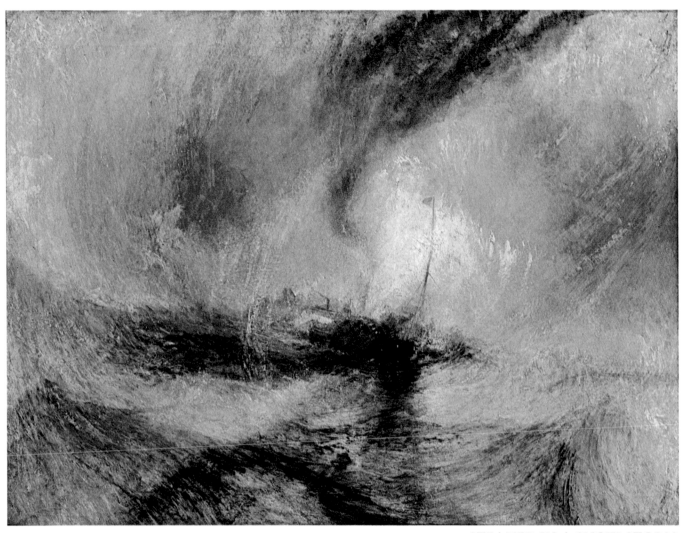

STEAMER IN A SNOW STORM

But Turner's subjects are often traditional. *Ulysses Deriding Polyphemus* illustrates a subject from Homer's *Odyssey:* in the golden glow of sunset, Trojan ships escape under the shadow of the threatening giant who looms above them like a storm cloud. Tragedy approaches melodrama in *The Slave Ship* which, foundering in a storm, has been lightened by throwing helpless captives overboard. A welter of bodies, arms and legs is dimly seen in the seething water.

Turner caught with his brush the true character of water. Waves have weight and power. Ships are borne firmly and behave correctly under the impact of wind and sea. To insure accuracy he spent four hours bound to the mast of a ship in a winter storm before painting *Steamer in a Snow Storm.* When critics said the picture looked like "soap suds and white wash," he said he wished they had been in it. The painting gives form to the force which is the essence of storm, and thus also anticipates modern Expressionism.

ÉDOUARD MANET

(1832–1883)

Rebel Against Tradition

PORTRAIT OF MANET,
BY EDGAR DEGAS

Like the scientist of the nineteenth century, the artist Édouard Manet was interested in the world around him. "One must be of one's time and paint what one sees," he wrote. Yet his paintings were the butt of perhaps the sharpest abuse ever directed at works of art.

Manet was born in Paris in 1832, the son of cultured and well-educated parents. His father, a government official, opposed an art career for his son, but when Édouard failed his examinations for the Navy, the elder Manet yielded.

Six years under a conservative teacher gave Manet an excellent technical training, and a reputation as a rebel. He insisted on using black and white as though they were colors. He took his models from the streets, dressed them in everyday clothes, and painted them, not with sympathy and understanding, but simply as they looked. The first painting he submitted to the Paris Salon, *The Absinthe Drinker,* showed a seedy drunkard who hung about the streets. The jury rejected it, of course, the first of many rejections. Both subject and method of painting offended them. Another early work, a large canvas called *The Old Musician,* brought together a group of models from "Little Poland," a Paris slum: a gypsy girl with a baby, two young boys, a genial old street violinist, the absinthe drinker again with tall hat and cape, and, half cut off as though by a badly aimed camera, a turbanned Saracen. No story connects these figures; they are simply put into one canvas and each is painted as the artist saw him.

Believing that the general public would understand better than the connoisseurs what he was trying to do, Manet in 1863 showed his paintings in a private gallery. But people were shocked, critics abusive. That year so many paintings were refused by the Salon (Manet's among them) that Napoleon III established a "Salon des Refusés" (that is, of the Rejects) where all could be shown. Crowds came, mostly to scoff, and Manet's paintings were the target of the most violent insults. Still hoping for understanding and approval, Manet at his own expense built for the Paris World's Fair of 1867 a pavilion in which to exhibit his works. "Every... painter in Paris turned up at the Manet exhibition," wrote a critic. "They all went wild with laughter."

Manet was deeply hurt. He wanted desperately to have his works appreciated, yet could not compromise his principles. His self-confidence was shaken. But younger men were rallying to

THE OLD MUSICIAN

him. On Friday evenings at the Café Guerbois two tables were reserved for a group of progressive thinkers, among them Manet and the artists Monet, Degas, Renoir, and Cézanne. Sometimes discussions were violent—one even led to a duel—but out of them came the color theories of Impressionism.

In his later years Manet finally received some public recognition. A number of his paintings were accepted for the Salon and one or two were even awarded medals. He was made a Chevalier of the Legion of Honor. But illness was creeping on him, and he died in 1883 at the age of fifty.

SOAP BUBBLES

"Paint What You See"

Why were Manet's paintings so sharply criticized? It is almost impossible for us in the twentieth century to understand, but the public in the 1860's was used to paintings that told stories, to interpretation of character in a face, or to some expression of feeling toward a subject. They liked warm, soft colors, whereas Manet's tones were often harsh. Their eyes were not trained to see things as they are. Manet's works looked ugly and vulgar.

Although primarily interested in recording directly what he saw around him, Manet also studied the results of what other people saw. In

the museums of Europe he admired the works of Velásquez and Frans Hals, both realists, and their use of black and gray. The flat areas of color edged by a black line in Japanese' prints reminded him of what he had already observed—that the eye does not actually see at a glance the subtle modeling from light to shade which was taught in the studios, but rather flat areas of color that turn abruptly to shadow. The newly invented camera also brought home this fact, sharpening the contrasts between lights and darks. In *Soap Bubbles* Manet patterns broad, almost shadowless areas of color against a dark ground.

Manet made few drawings. He wanted the finished work to maintain the intensity of his original idea and the freshness of a sketch. Describing his method, a friend said he "hurled himself on his bare canvas in a rush as though he had never painted before." Often at the end of a day's work, dissatisfied, he rubbed everything out.

Discussions in the Café Guerbois centered on what the eye really sees. Manet insisted that the artist look at nature and that he paint as he wishes in spite of academic rules. His own use of pure color formed a starting point. Gradually the Impressionist theory—that what one sees is colored light—was developed. Manet's style changed; his brush stroke became broader, his colors lighter and brighter. "M. Manet has been pleased to plaster his earth with violet mud," complained a critic in 1881. Of *Washday,* which was

THE PAVERS OF RUE DE BERNE

CLAUDE MONET IN HIS FLOATING STUDIO

painted in the new style, Manet said, "One can feel the air circulating around the woman and child." Similarly, *The Pavers of Rue de Berne* is flooded with sunlight.

Manet was not an Impressionist. He never exhibited with the group, and he continued to use black, which the Impressionists said did not exist in nature. Yet he has been called "The Father of Impressionism." A remark of Degas after Manet's funeral is a fitting comment: "He was greater than we thought."

WASHDAY

When the aged Goya was in exile in France, he used to entertain his friends with tales of his wild youth. He had fled from home, he said, because of a fatal street fight; in Rome, caught in an escapade, he avoided the death penalty only through the intervention of the Spanish ambassador; one dark night in Madrid he had been knifed in the back. None of these stories can be documented and they are possibly the romancings of an old man, but they show that Goya wanted to be remembered as hot-headed and impetuous, taking full part in the life around him.

Francisco de Goya y Lucientes was born in a small town near Saragossa, Spain. When he was fourteen his father, a gilder, moved the family to the city and put the boy in school to learn drawing and painting. His talents developed slowly and his early works for local churches and monasteries are not remarkable. Twice he failed in a competition for a scholarship to the Madrid Academy. After studying in Italy for a time, Goya returned to Spain and became a designer of tapestries for the Royal Manufactory in Madrid. During the next seventeen years he painted more than sixty designs, learning to observe accurately and record quickly, with gay, fresh color and clear-cut lights and shadows suitable for use in tapestry. His connection with the Royal Manufactory admitted him to the royal art collections where he studied and copied works by the great masters. "I have had three teachers," he said later, "Velásquez, Rembrandt, and nature."

Through a brother-in-law who held the position of Painter to the King of Spain, Goya was introduced into court circles. He began to paint portraits and was soon officially appointed a court painter by Charles IV. *The Family of Charles IV*, painted in 1800, gathers into one large canvas the king, the queen, and eleven of their brothers, sisters, sons and daughters. The likenesses are penetrating and reveal Goya's wit and satire, for the king looks as he was, pompous and stupid, the queen, shallow and evil.

A severe illness in 1792 had left Goya stone deaf and subject to terrible headaches. Cut off by these afflictions from normal life, he gradually turned his attention to the weaknesses and abuses of society. In a series of etchings

FRANCISCO DE GOYA

(1746–1828)

Courage and Violence

SELF-PORTRAIT

Francisco de Goya

called *The Caprices* he criticized superstition, intolerance and frivolity. In another, *The Disasters of War,* drawn from scenes he witnessed during the French invasion, he protested vehemently, in brilliant and shocking compositions, against cruelty and injustice.

In the years following the French wars, bitterness and disillusion led Goya to produce large paintings filled with sinister figures—men, giants, beasts—creatures of his vivid imagination. Finally in 1824, disgusted with the new government which had imprisoned many of his friends, Goya left Spain to settle in France among other Spanish exiles. There, until his death, he continued to paint with vigor and originality.

FAMILY OF KING CHARLES IV

Revolution and Bull Ring

In the early years of the nineteenth century Napoleon was pushing his conquest of Europe. His armies met little resistance as they moved into Spain, for the people recognized the corruption of their government and hoped for reform. But on Sunday, May 2, 1808, the citizens of Madrid, disillusioned, rose in revolt against the foreign invader. Using knives, clubs and stones, they fought desperately but hope-lessly. As the night wore on, squads of French soldiers roamed the streets, dragging out and shooting suspected revolutionaries. Goya occupied an apartment where the street fighting was thickest and *The Executions of the Third of May* records what he himself may have witnessed: the shooting down of a band of helpless Spanish rebels.

Violence had always interested Goya. Throughout his long career he turned repeatedly to the bullfight as a subject for paintings and prints. This national sport

Francisco de Goya

AGILITY AND DARING OF JUANITO APIÑANI

CEBALLOS RIDING A BULL INTO COMBAT

of Spain appealed also to his love of pageantry and action. He knew it well. "I was a bullfighter in my youth," he claimed in his old age, having traveled with a company of bullfighters on his way to Italy. The acuteness of his observation and his accuracy in recording the postures of bulls, horses and men have been confirmed by modern high-speed photographs.

Unusual in composition is *The Bullfight*. Parallel bands of spectators are connected by the diagonal fence cutting the ring. A counter diagonal, tying the two halves together, is made by bull and fighters. Other groups balance, right and left. Each bull, silhouetted against light ground, is painted carefully, while men and spectators are brushed in with swift, seemingly careless strokes. Goya was an Impressionist sixty years before Impressionism.

In a series of etchings, Goya presented famous fighters in episodes in the ring. *The Agility and Daring of Juanito Apiñani in the Madrid Plaza* shows the toreador vaulting over the bull's horns. Another

ACCIDENT IN THE MADRID PLAZA

THE BULLFIGHT

BOYS WITH JACKKNIVES

print shows *Mariano Ceballos Riding a Bull into Combat with Another in the Madrid Plaza*. Although the prints were made long after the events they record, the titles read like captions in a current newspaper. One of the most striking is Goya's report of *An Unfortunate Accident in the Bleachers of the Madrid Plaza and the Death of the Mayor of Torrejón*. It happened at a bullfight held in honor of the accession of Charles IV in 1789. The powerful shape against the blank sky is made more shocking by being off-center: bull and seething crowd balanced against emptiness.

JAN VERMEER

(1632–1675)

A "Little Master"

It is fitting that a self-portrait of Vermeer should show only his back. Little is known of him beyond a few official records. Not one letter or personal comment has been found to throw light on his family life, character or methods. After his death his paintings were often attributed to other artists. His works began to attract notice in the nineteenth century at the same time as did those of the French Impressionists, perhaps because he, too, was concerned with the painting of light.

Johannes van der Meer, called Jan Vermeer, was born in Delft in 1632, the son of a silk weaver and art dealer who also ran a tavern. The family lived in a house on the market square with weaving rooms upstairs and the tavern below, its walls offering space for the display of paintings for sale.

Jan was admitted to the painters' guild in 1653, but we do not know with whom he had served his apprenticeship. Delft, a center for the manufacture of china, was prosperous in the seventeenth century and boasted many good artists. One was a witness at Jan's marriage, and others must have frequented the tavern, perhaps marketing their paintings there.

The death of his father the year after Vermeer became a master painter left him the care of his mother, his wife, the house and the business. Twenty years later his own death is recorded. The register mentions his wife and eleven children, eight of them under twenty-one. The inventory of his estate lists studio furniture and costumes, easels, paints and paintings. Shortly afterward his wife declared bankruptcy. Three of Jan's paintings had gone to the baker in part payment of bills for bread; another, probably *The Artist in His Studio,* was given to his mother-in-law in return for a loan. A year later twenty-six paintings were sold at auction for a small sum.

Yet now Vermeer is regarded as one of the greatest of Dutch artists. The small number of his canvases (only thirty-six survive) and their high prices, led the forger Van Meegeren in the 1930's to forge Vermeers—he claimed he had found them—which he sold profitably until the fraud was uncovered.

The artist shown in Vermeer's picture is painting "Fame," or perhaps "History," laurel-crowned, a trumpet in one hand, and a gold-covered book on her arm. He has sketched the figure lightly in chalk and is laying color on the wreath. Is the painting merely a record of Vermeer at work? Perhaps, but more probably it is an allegory of the painter who, himself mortal, seeks immortality through the creations of his mind and brush.

THE ARTIST IN HIS STUDIO

THE CONCERT

LADY READING A LETTER

The Dutch at Home

Vermeer was born, lived, and died in Delft. One of his few outdoor paintings shows a bit of the city with its gables, chimneys, spires and turrets patterned against the wide Dutch sky. But most of his paintings are set indoors and show his remarkable ability to see and record light coming from a single source, picking up details of objects and modifying in intensity as it flows over wall and ceiling.

The *Lady Reading a Letter* may be Vermeer's young wife. She appears often, wearing this same black and gold dress which was apparently a studio property. Here, she stands in the light flooding through the open window, her intent face reflected in the glass. The diagonal of chair and window, the rumpled table cover and tipped fruits help to define the space of the picture. From a rod across the top hangs a silk curtain. A heavier curtain is looped up in *The Artist in His Studio*. Did Vermeer use this device to indicate that he was painting a scene from its reflection in a mirror from which the protecting curtain has been pushed back? Many artists of the seventeenth century experimented with mirrors and the new "camera obscura." The latter, an ancestor of our camera, was a dark box in which, through the use of lenses, a small image of a scene was projected on a mirror. If Vermeer used such tools it would help to explain the quality of his light.

Vermeer is one of the Dutch "little masters," so-called because their paintings were small enough to be hung in private houses. *The Lacemaker* measures only eight by ten inches. Here the light comes from the right, falling on the figure and the back wall, which is darker where face and dress are light, and brighter behind the hair and sleeve.

In *The Concert* performers on spinet and lute

THE LACEMAKER

accompany a woman who beats time as she sings. The curves of figures, table cover, raised lid of the instrument and viola da gamba contrast with the rectangles of pictures, chairs and angled floor tiles. Again, light bathes the scene.

But Vermeer is perhaps most famous for his handling of color. Over two hundred years after his death another Dutch artist, Vincent van Gogh, wrote to a friend, "Do you know a painter called Jan van der Meer?... The palette of this strange artist comprises blue, lemon-yellow, pearl gray, black and white. It is true that in the few pictures he painted one can find all the colors. But the combination of lemon-yellow, a dull blue and a light gray is... characteristic of him." "This strange artist"—a curious phrase to use of an artist whose subjects are so easy to recognize. Yet one cannot look long at his paintings without feeling this strangeness, as though the scene were permanently fixed in a crystal box.

WILLIAM HOGARTH

(1697–1764)

Social Commentator

SELF-PORTRAIT WITH DOG

Is there a "line of beauty"? William Hogarth believed he had found it in the flattened S-curve which appears on the palette below his self-portrait. In a treatise on painting called *The Analysis of Beauty* he discussed his art theories. From early childhood, he tells us, he had been interested in art, even leaving his play to watch a neighboring painter. His father, a poor schoolmaster, apprenticed him to an engraver, and at twenty-three he opened a business of his own, engraving signs and book illustrations.

To improve his drawing, Hogarth entered an art academy, but he was not a good student. Impatient with the formal classes, he sketched people on the streets in the activities of daily life, coming to class only occasionally to check his handling of anatomy. This independence of spirit, together with ready wit and a sharp-tongued honesty that approached rudeness, cost him friends, but also created the social and political satires which, in the form of engravings, secured him a life-long income.

But Hogarth wanted to be a painter. He studied further by himself and with Sir James Thornhill, an artist friend whose daughter he married. He became proficient in portraiture, having an uncanny ability to catch a likeness and to render easy and natural poses. Possibly invented by him were the small group portraits, sometimes no more than a foot high, called "conversation pieces," which became popular in eighteenth century England. These show a family or group of friends in a living room, garden, or other appropriate setting. An unusual example represents Captain George Graham and his staff after dinner in a cabin aboard ship. Men, servants, and even the dogs, one of which is wearing a wig, are joining in a musical number.

Hogarth scorned social pretense and sought no favors, but he was gratified when in his later years he was appointed Sergeant-Painter to King George II.

MARRIAGE À LA MODE, SCENE I: MARRIAGE CONTRACT (Below, a detail)

MARRIAGE À LA MODE, SCENE IV: THE LEVÉE

Life in Eighteenth-Century England

Hogarth is best known for his satires on English life—picture stories often with a moral. In *The Progress of Cruelty,* for instance, the boy who begins by tormenting his dog ends by killing his wife. In the series on the fashionable marriage, the young couple who marry for money and title end by dying miserably from the result of their selfishness.

Scenes are crowded with details interesting for what they show of the life of the times as well as for their importance to the story. The first scene of *Marriage à la Mode* takes place in a stuffy but luxurious room where the Earl of Squanderfield, a nobleman short of money, and a rich merchant eager for a title, are arranging the marriage of a son and a daughter. Young Lord Squanderfield at the left, fashionably dressed, takes snuff and looks at himself in a mirror. His sulky bride swings her ring while she listens to the flirtatious whisperings of Councilor Silvertongue. The bewigged and gouty earl displays his family tree springing from William the Norman, while the merchant peers through his glasses to check the terms of the contract.

In *The Enraged Musician* a foreign violinist, bow in hand, tries frantically to close his ears to the din of street noises. A beggarwoman with a baby is singing. A little girl twirls a noisemaker and a small boy clatters a tile over the cobblestones. Another beats a drum. A man walks by practicing his oboe. A fish-girl's bell, a hog-catcher's horn, a street vendor's bawling and a knife grinder's wheel add to the ear-splitting racket. On the roof two cats fight. Even the pretty milkmaid, pail on head, is calling for customers.

Hogarth weaves every detail into a unified whole. We enjoy the story, we delight in the glimpses of life in the eighteenth century. But the paintings live because of the artist's handling of the essentials of good art: drawing, color and design.

LORD GEORGE GRAHAM IN HIS CABIN

THE ENRAGED MUSICIAN

LEONARDO DA VINCI

(1452–1519)

Man of Genius

SELF-PORTRAIT

Legends developed about Leonardo da Vinci even during his own lifetime: his handsome face and figure, his strength and athletic prowess, his gentleness to animals and birds, his brilliance of mind, and the variety and scope of his talents. For Leonardo was one of the most gifted men who ever lived. He was first of all a painter, but he was also architect, sculptor, engineer and musician. He designed costumes and stage sets for pageants; he worked as a military engineer; he wrote a *Treatise on Painting;* he prepared text and illustrations for books on the anatomy of men and of horses; he made diagrams for an important book on mathematics. He was accepted as an equal by the most learned men of his time, was friend to the rulers of Florence, Milan, and Rome, and died in the service of the King of France.

Called by the name of the little town of Vinci where he was born, Leonardo grew up in Florence, a city teeming with men of ideas and with interest in the arts. His education was modest, but in the workshop of Verrocchio, painter and sculptor, where he served his apprenticeship, he had opportunity not only to learn his craft, but to listen to the scholars and noblemen who came to order works of art.

Leonardo's paintings include portraits, mythological themes and religious subjects. His *The Last Supper,* located in the dining room of a monastery in Milan, has deteriorated seriously over the years. During World War II only a bank of sandbags saved it when the room was struck by a bomb. Now, cleaned and restored, we at least see the masterly composition in which the artist focuses attention on a quiet Christ, while the men around him assume characteristic postures: tense Judas drawing back on the left, gentle John fainting in grief, impetuous Peter pushing between Judas and John as he asks, "Is it I who will betray you?"

Two versions exist of the *Virgin of the Rocks,* one in Paris and one in London, both probably painted by Leonardo or under his direction. Mary kneels behind the group, her wide cloak enclosing John the Baptist and Jesus. One hand hovers over her son, the other rests on the little St. John. Behind the Christ Child is an angel. The soft beauty of the faces—whether wistful, serene, or yearning—is painted with great subtlety.

Leonardo traveled from one end of Italy to the other as well as into France, working on, but seldom completing, projects in engineering, fortification, painting and sculpture. He was dogged by complaining letters and lawsuits for not fulfilling his contracts. His fellow-Florentine, Michelangelo, taunted him with "horse-modeler that thou art, unable to cast a statue in bronze," when he abandoned work on an equestrian statue of the Duke of Milan. But even though unfinished, Leonardo's works are among the most famous in the world, and his drawings and diagrams reveal one of the great creative geniuses of all time.

VIRGIN OF THE ROCKS

THE LAST SUPPER

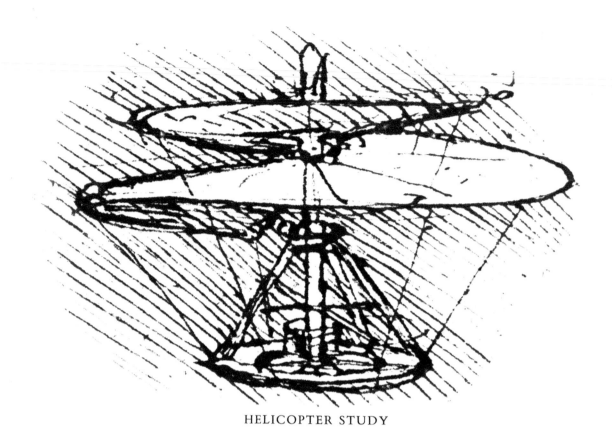

HELICOPTER STUDY

Scientist and Inventor

TANK (RIGHT SIDE UP)

Leonardo believed that an artist must understand the structure of objects, whether mountains, plants, animals, buildings, or men, in order to paint them successfully. His curiosity and acute observation led him into scientific analyses far beyond the ordinary needs of most painters or sculptors. The breadth of his interest and the progress of his studies are seen in more than thirty large notebooks containing drawings and notes of what he saw and thought. The notes,

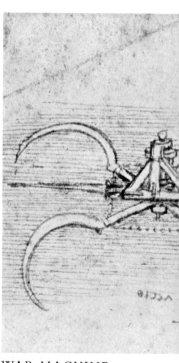

WAR MACHINE

oddly enough, are written backward with his left hand —why, no one knows—so that they have to be read in a mirror. Here are sketches for works of art intermingled with studies of flowers, rocks, storm clouds and whirlpools, of the anatomy of men and animals, of buildings, and of engineering projects. Leonardo apparently was able to see more acutely than others. His drawings of how birds fly anticipate the discoveries brought about by the slow-motion movie camera. This interest in the flight of birds led him to design a kind of glider in which a man could flap wings and steer. In fact he came

PARACHUTE

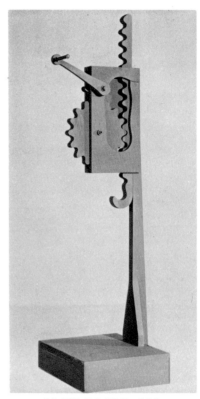

JACK BASED ON
LEONARDO DESIGN

BIRDS IN FLIGHT

CARICATURE OF FIVE HEADS

closer to inventing a flying machine than anyone up to modern times.

Some of Leonardo's most interesting inventions were in the field of military engineering. He designed a tank, armed with guns, which could be maneuvered by men on foot inside it. He worked out new ways of raising the muzzle of a cannon in order to aim it accurately. His sketches for drawbridges, for two-level street traffic, for a lifting device similar to the automobile jack, for a scaling ladder like that now used by fire-fighters, for a type of machine gun—to mention only a few—are so complete and accurate that working models of them have been made and exhibited in our own times.

DESIGN FOR STATUE

STUDY FOR THE LEDA

AN ANTIQUE WARRIOR

73

AUGUSTE RODIN

(1840–1917)

Dreamer and Creator

In their search for ways to show light and air, the Impressionists produced brilliant records of weather and times of day, but people became merely objects reflecting light. Influenced by the same scientific point of view, sculptors of the same period became content with mere accuracy of anatomy and costume. The loss of personality and character in the representation of human beings disturbed the young sculptor, Auguste Rodin. He worked to combine accurate anatomy and surface light and shadow, and at the same time to express the inner nature of man.

Born in Paris in 1840 (the same year as Monet), Rodin, at fourteen, entered a school of industrial arts, where he learned to draw from memory and became interested in sculpture. But he developed slowly, and during the 1860's and 1870's he produced what he later called "the sins of my youth" in the popular style which copied nature exactly.

IN RODIN'S STUDIO, A PHOTOGRAPH BY EDWARD STEICHEN

The death of his sister in 1862 affected Rodin deeply. For a time he thought of becoming a monk, but the head of the order which he entered recognized his artistic talent and dissuaded him. He married and had a son. During the war with Germany in 1871 he served in the National Guard, and afterward, in the troubled period following the French defeat, he left his family in Paris and worked in Belgium. He became obsessed with the suffering, the frustration, the tragedy of human life, and devoted himself to finding ways to express this in sculpture.

A trip to Italy in 1875 introduced Rodin to the works of Michelangelo. At home, he toured French cathedrals studying their sculpture. In museums he saw the marble and bronze figures of ancient Greece and Rome. Gradually his style developed. To combine the energy of Michelangelo, the fervor of Gothic saints, the accuracy of the Greeks, the flickering light of the Impressionists, and at the same time to express deep human emotion, became his goal.

Work was Rodin's life. He spent years on each major sculpture, making hundreds of sketches, dozens of plaster models. Many of his works gave rise to bitter controversy because of poses, costumes, or treatment. Yet almost from the beginning the artist received recognition. His works were exhibited widely; many were bought by the State.

Rodin's greatest project, bronze doors for the Museum of Decorative Arts in Paris, occupied him more than twenty years and was left unfinished at his death. Nearly two hundred figures were made for these "Gates of Hell," inspired by Dante's *Inferno*. At the top, leaning forward, his head on his hand as though pondering the problem of life and death, is *The Thinker*, Rodin's best known work. Many years after the original clay model was completed, some friends had a large version cast in bronze and placed in front of the Pantheon in Paris. Another cast stands outside the Hotel Biron, Rodin's Paris studio, now a museum of his works. A third marks Rodin's grave in the garden of his country home at Meudon. To many the figure has become a symbol of the dawn of thought. To Rodin it stood for the artist, both dreamer and creator.

THOUGHT

Spirit in Stone and Bronze

Two ways of producing sculpture have been in use since earliest times. In one the artist *takes away* from a mass of material until the figure has been "found" within the block. In the other he begins with a foundation of cardboard or wire and *builds up* the figure out of blobs of soft clay. To make a fragile clay figure last, however, it must be translated into durable material. A mold into which melted metal can be poured is made from the clay model. Every detail of the original will appear in the metal and several casts exactly alike can be made from the same mold. Sometimes the artist polishes the surface himself; sometimes this is done by metal workers.

BURGHERS OF CALAIS

Rodin used both processes. In *Thought*, which was made by chipping away the stone, he left part of the block uncut, contrasting the smooth finish of the head with the rough marble. *The Thinker, The Age of Bronze* and *The Burghers of Calais* were modeled in clay and then cast in bronze. Rodin left the surfaces rough, showing the lumps of clay and even the marks of the mold, so that the process of creation would remain visible.

Perhaps inspired by his war experience, Rodin's first major work was *The Con-*

quered. A young Belgian soldier served as model. Muscles and flesh are so accurate that the artist had trouble persuading critics he had not merely taken a cast of an actual human figure. Admirers renamed the work *The Age of Bronze,* seeing in it the struggle of mankind to rise from the animal level to spiritual awareness.

The Burghers of Calais was commissioned by the French seaport to commemorate a heroic moment in its history. For eleven months in 1346 the English had besieged Calais until disease and starvation

AGE OF BRONZE

WEEPING BURGHER

drove the citizens to ask for terms of surrender. King Edward III agreed to spare the town if six of its leading men would submit themselves to him in sackcloth, barefoot, with ropes around their necks. A chronicler describes how the six volunteers, led by the elderly merchant Eustache de Saint Pierre, crossed to the enemy camp and knelt before the king. The English nobles, moved by their courage, pleaded for mercy, but Edward spared the burghers only when his queen begged him for their lives.

In the sculpture, resolve, resignation, despair, fear are expressed in faces and bodies—even in the draperies. Rugged surfaces with lumps and hollows that reflect or hold the light, angular poses and exaggerated hands and feet add to the dramatic effect.

Rodin repeatedly asserted his devotion to nature: "I present nature exactly as she is." But what of the exaggerations so obvious in *The Burghers?* "I see all the truth, not only that of the outside," said Rodin. "I reproduce the spirit."

SELF-PORTRAIT

A VENETIAN LADY

ALBRECHT DÜRER

(1471–1528)

Master of Detail

A link between the artistic thought and craftsmanship of north Europe and Italy in the sixteenth century is the German artist Albrecht Dürer, who in ability and variety of accomplishment can be ranked with the great geniuses of the Renaissance.

Dürer was born in Nuremberg and received his early training from his father, an immigrant Hungarian goldsmith, whose shop he entered as soon as he learned to read. There he acquired skill in engraving directly on metal, useful later when he mastered a new process whereby a picture could be printed from lines scratched in the surface of a copper plate. These lines, filled with ink and squeezed against wet paper, produced an impression which could be sold for a moderate price. Another method of making cheap pictures was practiced in the shop of Wolgemut, to whom Dürer was apprenticed to learn painting. Parts to print white were gouged out of a piece of plank, its surface then inked and stamped on paper. Many copies of a picture could be produced from one original plate or block. Under Wolgemut, the boy Dürer not only mastered the craft of painting but assisted with the woodcut illustrations for the *Nuremberg Chronicle,* a sort of illustrated encyclopedia, which was printed in 1493. At nineteen, then, his apprenticeship over, Dürer knew how to engrave, paint, and make woodcuts.

Four years of travel—to the Netherlands to see the painting of Jan van Eyck and his followers, through Germany and Switzerland to learn from artists whose fame had reached him—continued Dürer's education. A year after his return to Nuremberg (and shortly after his marriage), he went to Italy, a visit repeated eleven years later when he stayed in Venice for eighteen months, honored by nobility, envied by artists. "How I shall long for this sun when I am back in the cold," he wrote a friend. "Here I am a gentleman, at home a parasite."

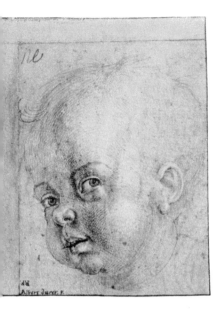

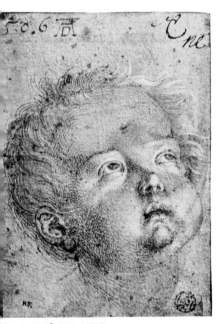

BABIES' HEADS

Back in Nuremberg, Dürer produced many paintings and his greatest prints. He studied languages and mathematics and began a treatise on the theory of art. He was honored with a pension by Emperor Maximilian I. In 1520–21, with his wife, he visited the Netherlands to sell prints, to secure the patronage of Maximilian's successor, Charles V, and for pleasure and information. His fame had preceded him and he was honored with receptions, dinners, gifts. His diary with its account of his doings, sketches of things he saw, and detailed record of his expenses gives us an insight into the times, and into his own gracious but precise and careful nature. He returned home refreshed, but he had contracted malaria on a trip to see a whale, and the disease eventually caused his death.

Dürer drew and painted himself many times. At twenty, his intent and penetrating gaze under the shadowing hand suggests the restless curiosity that made possible his great work.

WEEPING CHERUB

APOSTLE

The Wonders of Nature

FANTASTIC RHINOCEROS

Dürer's industry was enormous. Besides making some seventy paintings and hundreds of engravings and woodcuts, he wrote and illustrated books on geometry, fortifications and human proportions. But some of his most charming works, known at the time only to himself and a few friends, are his drawings, more than a thousand of which survive.

Insatiable curiosity about everything—commonplace or unusual, large or small, man-made or natural—prompted his pen, brush and silverpoint—a fine wire used before the invention of the modern pencil. Men and women, rich and poor, old and young, happy and sad, meet on the pages of his notebooks. A baby could serve as a cherub head. Costume designs might be useful in scenes of saints. Animals both domestic and strange were endlessly fascinating. The description of a rhinoceros sent to the king of Portugal led Dürer to draw a fantastic creature with skin resembling medieval armor. In *Knight, Death and the Devil*, a hog-snouted Devil and a worm-riddled Death on a skinny horse accompany the steadfast rider. Skull, lizard and dangling roots contribute to the sense of evil.

DECORATION FOR PRAYER BOOK

HARE

RABBITS

KNIGHT, DEATH AND THE DEVIL

COLUMBINE

The care lavished on every hair of rabbit's fur, every flower and blade of grass, every line of hand or face approached religious fervor in Dürer as it had with Jan van Eyck a century earlier. It stemmed from a reverence for all creation and a faith that the artist as creator shares in the creativity of God. But the sixteenth century was stirred also by a scientific spirit which drove men to seek understanding for its own sake. Like his Italian contemporary, Leonardo da Vinci, Albrecht Dürer was in this sense a true son of the Renaissance.

WINSLOW HOMER

(1836–1910)

Reporter in Paint

Always observant of the world around him, Winslow Homer was the forerunner of the modern news photographer when, during the Civil War, he was sent to the front as a war correspondent. Drawings of soldiers and their life in field and camp, which he sent back, were transferred by hand to wood blocks and printed in *Harper's Weekly,* the popular magazine of the time. Photography was in its infancy and Homer used pencil and brush instead of camera. He had the essentials for success: a discerning eye, skill and speed in drawing, a feeling for the news value of an incident, a sense of humor, and human sympathy. In *A Rainy Day in Camp,* a scene of army

STUDY OF A SOLDIER

A RAINY DAY IN CAMP

THE HERRING NET

misery—poignant because so commonplace—is relieved by the painting of light and air and by the touch of humor in the uncomfortable burro, staked apart from the other animals.

Homer was a New Englander. His father ran a hardware store in Boston; his mother, who had "a pretty talent for painting flowers in watercolor," came from Maine. The boy began to draw as soon as he could hold a pencil. At nineteen he was apprenticed to a lithographer, and later did free-lance illustrating, but his formal art training was scanty.

In 1864, Homer exhibited several paintings at the National Academy and at twenty-nine he was made a member. A trip to Europe did not change his style or his interest in the American scene. From boyhood he had loved the country; his subject matter is drawn from the life of the farm, the school, the small town. A gentle humor, warmth toward people, especially women and children, and a hint of story share in the appeal of his painting.

During a winter in England he became fascinated by the violence of the sea, and in 1884 he moved to Prout's Neck, Maine, where he built himself a cottage on the cliffs over-looking the ocean. There, with interludes of fishing and hunting in the north woods, and wintering in the Caribbean, he lived alone for the rest of his life, seeing few people, doing his own cooking and housework, and continuing to paint.

The Sea

Winslow Homer's ideal of art perfectly fitted nineteenth-century taste. "When I have selected the thing carefully, I paint it exactly as it appears," he said. This was essentially the theory of all nineteenth-century realists. Why, then, do the works of Homer look so different from those of Monet, for instance? To Monet the thing "as it appears" meant *at a given moment,* with all the accidents of light and weather that occurred at that particular time. Monet concluded that his subject, then, was really colored light, and developed a way of painting it with small blobs of bright paint. Homer, on the other

BREEZING UP

hand, sometimes worked on a subject for years, painting swiftly, but laying the canvas aside for long intervals. He built a studio on runners, with a plate glass window, so that he could push it to the view he wanted and study it in all weathers. He would select essentials, leaving out cluttering detail. He had an unusual ability to see and record light and atmosphere and an instinct for design. In the finished work he gathered memories of many aspects of a view, giving the spectator a sense of sharing in it.

Pleasure boating is the theme of *Breezing Up,* which shows a small boat scudding before a rising breeze. Heeling hull, boiling wake, and cut-off sail give the sense of speed so dear to sailors. More serious in mood is *The Herring Net,* where men who make a living from the sea hunch over their shimmering catch. Mists shroud the distant ships, and dark sky and rolling waves in the sunset light warn of a stormy night. In his late paintings Homer omits people entirely, and devotes himself to recording the majesty, the power and the loneliness of the sea.

One of Homer's important contributions to American art was his handling of watercolor. Before the nineteenth century the medium had served only for studies and sketches but Homer, like Turner in England, used it for finished works. With it he caught the brilliance of changing sun and air.

THE PAINTER AND THE CONNOISSEUR

PIETER BRUEGEL

(About 1525–1569)

Life in Flanders

Pieter Bruegel must have started with high spirits on his long journey south, for Rome was the art center of the world in the sixteenth century. Of peasant background, and having only recently finished his apprenticeship, he would have traveled mostly on foot the more than eight hundred miles up the Rhine valley, across the Alps and down into Italy. In his boyhood he probably walked the half-day's journey from Brögel, the north Flemish village which gave him his name, to 'sHertogenbosch to see the fantasies painted by Jerome Bosch. His early works show the influence of those paintings. Later, in

Antwerp, his master, Pieter Coeck, had brought to his attention the new ideas coming from Italy. Now he had a chance to study them for himself.

Young Bruegel visited Rome and probably Venice and Naples, but apparently he was little interested in the recently completed masterpieces of such artists as Tintoretto and Michelangelo. He brought back with him sketches of river valleys and mountains, of castles, villages and forests, and a love for wide views from mountain heights. In his later paintings he sometimes included buildings that remind one of Italy, but his people, his subjects, and his way of painting remained thoroughly Flemish.

Returning to Antwerp, Bruegel assisted in a print shop for a time; then, in 1563, he married and settled in Brussels. Two sons, Pieter the Younger and Jan, both became painters, though they could not have learned from their father for he died when they were small children.

Bruegel liked to picture events from the Bible as though they were happening in his own day and in his own home town. *The Arrival in Bethlehem,* a scene from the life of Christ, takes place among steep-roofed Flemish houses on the bank of a frozen stream. The sun is setting over a cold, snowy landscape. People go about their business, carrying loads across the ice, warming themselves at a fire. Children work or play or fight. In the inn the light shows where the tax collector is gathering his dues. Servants kill a hog to provide food for the many visitors. And Mary and Joseph arrive quietly with their ox and ass. Tomorrow will bring the joy of the first Christmas, but today nobody notices; they are just people among people in this busy winter scene.

TWO BURGHERS

Peasants at Work and Play

Bruegel is best known for his scenes of peasant life. Although in Antwerp and Brussels he moved among educated people, he felt at home with peasants and enjoyed mingling with them at weddings, country dances, and at their daily labor. His drawings and paintings show acute observation and a rare ability to indicate, through the line surrounding flat areas of color, both the solidity of figures and their capacity for movement. Shadows are omitted and faces represent types rather than individuals. Some are close to caricature.

In *The Peasant Wedding* Bruegel shows peasants at the important business of eating and drinking. The bride who sits in the place of honor under the bridal crown seems wrapped in herself, apart; broad-backed young men bring in pies on a shutter; a helpful guest passes them down the table. The stubby little child in the foreground beside the wine jugs sets the mood for the whole—the concentration on eating.

Another scene of peasant life shows a stout bagpiper screwing up his face in mock agony as a youth teasingly offers a jug of wine that he cannot possibly drink while he blows. Behind him, men quarrel and lovers kiss; opposite, a man leads his partner into the dance; in the corner, two little girls dance together.

Toward the end of his career Bruegel began a series of paintings to illustrate the activities that take place in each month of the year. Such scenes were often carved on the portals of Gothic cathedrals or painted in the calendars of illuminated prayer books. The subject for February was usually people warming themselves. Bruegel accepted the familiar theme, but made of it one small incident in his painting—at the left, under the inn sign. For him, *February* meant winter itself. Hunters and shivering dogs, black against the

THE ARRIVAL IN BETHLEHEM

Pieter Bruegel

PEASANT WEDDING

FEBRUARY: HUNTERS IN THE SNOW

PEASANT DANCE

white, trackless snow, plod up the
slope. Bare branches with a few
bleak birds twist against the pale sky.
Below stretch snowy fields and
frozen ponds dotted with people.
A wagon moves along a tree-lined
road. Steep-roofed houses, clustered
here and there about a church, lead
one on under a towering crag to a
town on the shore of a sea or lake,
pearly in the distant light. Such
a view belongs, not to Bruegel's
flat Netherlands, but to the upper
Rhine or the Austrian Alps.

REMBRANDT VAN RIJN

(1606–1669)

Man's Inner Self

SELF-PORTRAIT

Few would question the statement that Rembrandt van Rijn was among the greatest of painters. But about his relations with friends and pupils, his reputation during his lifetime and his character, there are wide differences of opinion.

Many facts are documented. Rembrandt was born in Leyden in 1606, son of a well-to-do miller, Harmen van Rijn. The boy went to the local grammar school, and then, briefly, to the university; he was determined to become an artist. A three-year apprenticeship to a local painter gave him the technical background, and a brief period in Amsterdam with an Italian-trained artist brought him into contact with the style of the late Renaissance. But Rembrandt, though he admired Italian art, was bent on painting in his own way.

Holland's flourishing trade in the seventeenth century brought increased population to her cities, and wealth to her middle class. Bankers, merchants, city officials wanted portraits of themselves and their families. In Amsterdam Rembrandt found plenty of commissions and soon was surrounded with pupils. Marriage to Saskia van Uylenburgh, the orphaned daughter of a wealthy burgomaster, brought him position and fortune. The young couple bought an imposing house with sleeping quarters and studios for pupils, and space for the works of art, curios and studio properties which Rembrandt liked to collect. In spite of a large income, debts began to pile up.

Rembrandt was at the height of his powers and success. A Leyden historian in 1641 spoke of him as "one of the most famous painters of our century." In 1642 he delivered to the Great Hall of the Musketeers' Guild in Amsterdam the *Sortie of Captain Banning Cocq's Company,* later called the *Night Watch,* which one of his pupils described as "so powerful that all the other pieces there stand beside it like mere playing-card pictures."

But the death of three children in infancy, followed by that of his wife in 1642, left Rembrandt alone with a fourth child, Titus, only nine months old. His self-portraits at this point show his face heavy with grief. Problems multiplied. Debt, and Saskia's will which left him her property only so long as he remained single, probably prevented his marrying Hendrickje Stoffels, a kindly servant girl who managed his household.

Rembrandt withdrew more and more into himself. He still had many commissions, both private and official, and during the 1640's and 1650's produced some of his finest works, in etching as well as painting. But his financial affairs became still more tangled. In 1656 he was declared bankrupt, and two years later his house and all his property were sold, including his collections. Hendrickje and Titus helped support the family by opening a shop for the sale of Rembrandt's prints and paintings.

Hendrickje died in the early 1660's and Titus a few years later. Rembrandt, though his sight was failing, still painted with sure hand and rich color. That his fame had spread far is proved by a visit paid him in 1668 by a member of the Medici family, the Grand Duke of Tuscany, who bought one of the painter's self-portraits. A year later, noted only in the church register, is the record of Rembrandt's death. The cost of the funeral indicates an honorable burial, but the inventory of his personal property lists nothing but "some linen and woolen garments and his painting materials."

THE ARTIST'S WIFE, SASKIA

TITUS READING

OLD MAN WITH RED CAP

THE PANCAKE MAKER

TWO NEGROES

People of Amsterdam

Rembrandt was a tireless worker. Attributed to him are some six hundred paintings, between one and two thousand drawings and nearly three hundred etchings. Although his chief income probably came from portraits, he also painted themes from mythology and the Bible, landscapes and scenes of daily life.

A pupil described his methods. Contrary to what one would expect from the freedom and breadth of his brush strokes, he worked very slowly, requiring sittings over a two- or three-month period for each portrait. After the paint dried he would go over the surface again, using larger or smaller strokes until sometimes the paint built up to the thickness of half a finger.

Rembrandt was his own readiest model, and his many self-portraits make it possible

PORTRAIT OF JAN SIX

MAN IN A GOLD HELMET

THE ARTIST'S MOTHER

HENDRICKJE AT WINDOW

to note the changes in his appearance throughout his career. The eager, sharp-eyed boy became the prosperous man of 1640, richly dressed in the luxurious materials he loved to collect. Later portraits show him heavier, looking irritable and suspicious. He painted other members of his family: his mother, his beautiful wife Saskia, also dressed in the velvet and jewels which were studio properties. His older brother is shown wearing a gilded helmet from the collection. Later, we see the patient Hendrickje and the child Titus.

BEGGARS AT THE DOOR

We meet the people of Amsterdam: beggars going from door to door in coarse, ragged clothing, a wayside vendor cooking pancakes; two Negroes, who probably came to the city in the train of a visiting potentate. In the Jewish quarter near his home, Rembrandt studied the lined faces of bearded old men. The portrait of Jan Six, a stanch friend, shows us one of Amsterdam's most highly respected citizens, a collector, poet and dramatist who also served as burgomaster. During Rembrandt's hard years Six helped by commissioning numerous paintings and etchings. His house is now a museum of works by Rembrandt and contemporaries.

Interest in light, both natural and artificial, was characteristic of artists in the seventeenth century. Rembrandt observed light accurately, but was particularly concerned with using it to suggest mood. — It picks out the face and hands of a portrait, reflects from metal and jewelry, highlights silk or velvet. Both light and shadow are rich with color—yellow, red, brown, black. But most striking in Rembrandt's portraits is his respect for the privacy of the individual. They are convincing likenesses, vivid and full of character. They bring the sitter close to the spectator, almost within reach, yet through a shadow on the face or the lift of a shoulder Rembrandt reminds us that we never really know our fellow men.

Rembrandt's greatness rests almost as much on his drawings and etchings as on his paintings. With a few lines he establishes the setting, the posture of a figure, the expression of a face. As in his paintings, light and shadow play an important part. It is only through his whole work, staggering in its quantity, that we can grasp the breadth of his genius.

EDGAR DEGAS

(1834–1917)

Impressions of Light and Movement

SELF-PORTRAIT

At the race courses near Paris in the mid-nineteenth century the artist Edgar Degas was a familiar figure. Aloof from the spectators, unconcerned about winners, he concentrated on the movements of horses and jockeys. In the evenings at the theater he studied the ballet dancers, going backstage afterward to observe their weary postures. He had received a sound academic training in art and agreed with his teachers that line was more important than color. He practiced to make his drawing as sure as that of the great masters. How, then, did he come to join with the rebellious Manet and his friends at the Café Guerbois, to exhibit with them, to accept his share of the criticism launched against the Impressionists?

Edgar De Gas (he later abandoned this aristocratic form of the family name) was born in 1834, the son of a banker who provided him with an independent income. In spite of his academic training he managed, through many visits to the Louvre and a sojourn in Italy, to maintain a freshness of approach. From the fourteenth- and fifteenth-century Florentines he learned simple, effective silhouettes, fine modeling, and quiet color harmony. His early works were largely portraits of his family. Like the old masters he did not paint directly from the model but made sketches, then painted the portrait in his studio.

Degas had returned from Italy inspired to paint large historical pictures, but they were not successful. At this point in his career he met the group at the Café Guerbois. The discussions helped to free him from his attachment to the past and to turn his attention to the world around him. They opened his eyes to *color*. He exhibited with the group from 1874 to 1886.

A trip to New Orleans in 1873 to see his brothers, who were in business there, confirmed him in his love for Paris, where he withdrew more and more into himself. A bachelor, he lived in a large house on Montmartre, receiving only his models and a few friends, seldom going out except for daily walks. His eyes, which had always bothered him, were failing. He turned to sculpture, which he could *feel,* struggling with the problems of support and material, unwilling to ask advice. Because of faulty techniques many of his

Race Horses and Ballet Dancers

A GENTLEMAN RIDER

Degas maintained that art is a matter of the mind, not merely of the eye. He disliked painting outdoors, saying that an artist should *control* light, not be its servant. The aspect of the world that interested him most was *movement*. From the Impressionists he learned to draw with quick, shorthand strokes that gave the sense of motion, but he never lost his mastery of anatomy. He made it his task to reconcile the impressionist vision of the world one sees, with the intellectual standards of the art taught by the schools.

Degas was much influenced by Japanese prints with their strong contour lines, diagonal perspectives and views from odd angles. He was also interested in the camera and even became an amateur photographer. His canvases suggest the "candid" snapshot, catching people unposed. He began with an *idea* which he would then carry through by searching out and sketching the attitudes he wanted. The painting was created in the studio. "No art is less spontaneous than mine," he said, "which is wholly reflective."

Love of movement led Degas to the horse race and the ballet. He haunted both, observing and sketching. He had an amazingly acute eye and a photographic memory. He

works collapsed or disintegrated. Of some hundred and fifty pieces, perhaps half remained at his death. He also made a collection of paintings which included works by El Greco, the eighteenth-century masters, Ingres, Delacroix, Manet, and the Post-Impressionists.

Degas grew more eccentric. His wit, always sharp, became savage. He broke with his Impressionist friends. He wanted no honors and received none. Yet occasionally he showed his true self, full of self-doubt and a sense of failure. He worked furiously but, he said, "accomplishing nothing, finishing nothing."

Finally, in his eighties, almost completely blind and unable to paint, he walked the streets of Paris glimpsing shadows of the movement he loved. His death in 1917 during World War I was hardly noticed.

Edgar Degas

went behind the scenes, seeking "the unfamiliar aspects of the familiar." He was not interested in people—his jockeys have no personality, his dancers no feminine charm—but in the patterns they made against a background. Often a composition begins with a horse's hoof or a dancer's toe near the bottom of the canvas, then builds back with a series of zigzags and curves.

THE JOCKEYS

97

DANCER MASSAGING HER ANKLES

HIGH KICK

DANCER IN WHITE ON HER TOES

Through his contact with the Impressionists Degas became more and more interested in color. A portrait was described in 1883 as having "almost bright pink patches on the forehead, green on the beard... while the fingers are made up of yellow edged with... violet." He took up pastel because it gave him color and line together and produced both brilliance and softness. He studied new and daring light effects, especially on the stage.

With increasing blindness Degas' line became less precise, but he could

Edgar Degas

still see color. He piled up thick layers of pastel on his ballet dancers until they stand out from the paper, and he enriched the effect with strokes of pure orange or blue. Withdrawn though he was from the Paris of the twentieth century, the color of his late work holds its own with that of the Expressionists, who were making a practice of using color with similar violence.

TWO BALLET GIRLS

DIEGO VELÁSQUEZ

(1599–1660)

Painter to the King

SELF-PORTRAIT (DETAIL FROM
THE MAIDS OF HONOR)

On June 7, 1660, Maria Theresa, daughter of Philip IV of Spain, became the bride of Louis XIV of France. The event took place on a remote island in the river between the two countries. In charge of arrangements was the Palace Marshal, Gentleman of the King's Chamber, and Court Painter, Don Diego Velásquez. He supervised the journey from Madrid, the food and lodging for hundreds of courtiers and guests; he provided pageants at each of the stops en route; he brought fine furnishings to deck the marriage pavilion. Contemporary accounts describe his handsome figure in black, with a silver sword at his side and a heavy gold chain with the jeweled badge of office about his neck. But the work was taxing for a man of sixty-one. Velásquez returned exhausted to Madrid and died a few weeks later. The king, whose private physician had attended him, wrote on the margin of a document, "I am overwhelmed."

Born in Seville of noble parents, Velásquez, at eleven, was apprenticed to Pacheco, an artist, historian, and Inspector of Painting. Seven years later, shortly after passing the examinations that enabled him to set up as master painter, Velásquez married Pacheco's daughter. By the time he was nineteen he was employing two apprentices.

In 1623 Velásquez was invited to Madrid. A portrait he painted there of Philip IV so pleased the king that he made him Court Painter, with a regular salary, a studio in the palace, and a private residence in the city. King and painter became warm friends. A chair for the king, who liked to watch Velásquez at work and even practiced painting himself, was always ready in the artist's studio.

Encouraged by Rubens, who came from Flanders on a diplomatic mission, Velásquez visited Italy. There he stayed a year and a half studying the works of the great masters, especially Titian and Tintoretto. On a later trip he bought for Philip many of the paintings which are now the glory of the Prado Museum in Madrid.

In spite of such time-consuming official duties, Velásquez continued to paint. In *The Maids of Honor,* he brings us into his studio where five-year-old Princess Margarita faces her parents who are posing for their portrait. We glimpse them reflected in the mirror on the back wall. Two girls of noble rank frame the little princess. Court attendants gossip in the shadow; a dwarf pokes at a sleepy dog; another stares

THE MAIDS OF HONOR

amiably. The Queen's marshal looks back from the open doorway. Light plays softly over ceiling and walls, picks up the edge of the great canvas, and rests on the golden-haired child. At the left the painter himself, brush in hand, pauses in his work. On his breast gleams the red cross of a Knight of Saint James said to have been sketched there by the king himself when, two years after the canvas was completed, this highest honor was granted to Spain's great artist.

"SILVER PORTRAIT" OF PHILIP IV

Royalty and Courtiers

In the courts of Europe before the invention of photography, painted portraits were in great demand, especially for exchange with friendly rulers or to hang in palaces at home. Eligible princes and princesses were introduced to each other through likenesses brought by the envoys who arranged royal marriages.

Velásquez was kept busy. After that first successful portrait, Philip is said to have posed for no other artist. He was painted in the sober black garments of a Spanish grandee or in royal rose and silver, in hunting costume or on horse-back, a homely, but distinguished figure with Hapsburg jaw and fine blonde hair. The so-called "silver portrait," painted after Velásquez' first trip to Italy, shows the artist's firm drawing, quiet color, and paint laid on in dots and slashes that lose their meaning close up, but at a distance define clearly the forms and patterns.

For a royal hunting lodge outside Madrid, Velásquez produced a series of equestrian portraits, among them *Don Baltasar Carlos on Horseback*. Painted when the heir to the throne was only five, it shows the child solemnly imitating his father in pose and bearing, the royal baton in his hand. He bestrides his fat pony with the assurance of a skilled horseman (which he was), and from the spectator's eye level he towers against the sky. The colors are fresh, the cool blues and grays of the landscape setting off the warm vibrant tones of child and pony.

The death of Don Baltasar Carlos at sixteen left Philip without an heir. He then married Princess Mariana of Austria, who was only three years older than her step-daughter, Maria Theresa. Both—and later the Princess Margarita—appear often in the stiff, fashionable farthingales that made intimate portraiture difficult. But the artist managed, through silvery accents and touches of rose or blue, to give them life.

The last of the royal children to be painted by Velásquez was two-year-old Prince Felipe Prospero, a sickly baby who died a year later. His stiff, adult pose contrasts with that of the twisting puppy, and in his pale, serious little face Velásquez caught the wistful pathos of the frail child.

Perhaps no royal family was ever recorded with such sympathy and skill. Velásquez brought to the task an acute eye, an ability to translate into paint what he saw, a subtle color sense, plus respect and affection for his royal subjects.

DON BALTASAR CARLOS ON HORSEBACK

NFANTA MARIA THERESA THE COURT JESTER PRINCE FELIPE PROSPERO

JEROME BOSCH

(about 1450–1516)

Creator of Fantasies

SELF-PORTRAIT

A nightmare-world peopled with imps and demons, crippled and deformed, combining human, animal, bird, insect and fish forms, was created by the mind and brush of Jerome Bosch. Lacking scientific knowledge, Bosch believed that fires and floods, accidents and disease were caused by evil spirits in the world. They threatened people in every daily activity, even lurking in dark corners of the church. We find them still, carved in stone on medieval cathedrals or painted on the borders of medieval manuscripts.

Even worse than the devils that threatened from without were those that lived within men's hearts. Sinners who yielded to gluttony, drunkenness and vice might be enjoying themselves in this life but were doomed to eternal suffering. "Take warning," Bosch seems to say in his *Ship of Fools,* "You who are absorbed in eating, drinking and carousing are in a ship without a sail, with drunken jester for lookout. You must change your ways if you would reach port safely."

Few facts are known about Jerome van Aaken, who signed his paintings Jheronimus Bosch, using a Latin version of his first name and taking for surname the final syllable of 'sHertogenbosch, the town in Holland where he was born. A record of 1480 calls him "Jerome the Painter," which suggests that he was about thirty years old, for he would not have been so designated until he had finished his apprenticeship and achieved some recognition.

Bosch's paintings reveal no influence from the progressive artists of his century. His ideas grew out of the medieval belief in demons. As for his techniques, they appear to have come from the wall painting practiced in the small town, with its beautiful Gothic cathedral, where he spent his life and where his death is recorded in 1516.

A Nightmare World

SHIP OF FOOLS

Certain artists in our own day paint the world of dreams; Bosch was concerned with people awake but beset by evils, which appear in fantastic forms, engaged in all sorts of activities to afflict and terrify mankind.

In the legend of St. Anthony Abbot, Bosch found a hero for his fantasies. St. Anthony sold all his possessions and went into the desert for a life of poverty and prayer. But the memory of the good things he had given up tormented him. Devils, sometimes disguised as beautiful ladies, brought gold and silver, fine garments and rich foods to tempt him. When he refused them, they attacked him fiercely, lifting him up by the hair and beating him so severely that he was once found half dead. Healed, he taunted Satan, saying, "Here I am again to fight thee still." "Then was Satan furious," says the legend, "setting all his demons to try their powers to overcome him. They surrounded him with lions and tigers, serpents and scorpions and all the horrible shapes they could conceive, and they were roaring and hissing all around him." Suddenly there came a light from heaven and the voice of Christ saying, "Anthony, I am here beside thee." The beasts vanished.

In the center of Bosch's painting kneels St. Anthony. Strange creatures crowd in from all sides, each more gruesome than its neighbor. Sky and earth are alive with these terrifying shapes. That the saint will win over his tormentors we are assured by the scene above and to the right where, in a cavelike room, a tiny figure of Christ stands beside a crucifix. Thus Bosch makes his point that steadfast faith gives man power over evil.

The Temptation of St. Anthony is a triptych; its two outer panels were hinged to close over the central picture. On special occasions they were opened so that the faithful could see the evil and the victory over it, and feel hope for themselves, also.

THE TEMPTATION OF ST. ANTHONY (See details on facing page.)

PAINTERS

OF INDIA

(Mughal Period)

In the Royal Court

JAHANGIR RECEIVING A REPORT

In wave after wave, the fierce and ruthless Mongols swept over Asia in the Middle Ages, pressing their conquests into eastern Europe and south to the borders of Egypt. But the energies of the conquerors gradually turned to cultural pursuits. At the court of Persia (where they were called Mughals, or Moguls) they acquired tastes which they took to new capitals, building palaces with gardens of exotic plants and flowers, and menageries of wild beasts. Akbar, a warrior emperor who extended his control over most of India, also assembled a magnificent library. To copy and illustrate manuscripts, Persian painters—men of high birth—were invited to teach their skills in the State Academy at Fatehpur-Sikri. Akbar had studied painting in his youth and when he came to the throne in 1556 he personally supervised the more than a hundred artists, both Persian and Indian, in the palace studio.

Wall painting had been practiced in India from early times, and after paper was introduced from China in the fourteenth century, miniature painting became equally popular. But the spread of Mohammedanism discouraged the making of pictures; to create men and animals in paint was to rival God, said the priests, and to risk punishment on the Day of Judgment. The court was powerful enough, however, to stand against such superstition. "Only bigoted followers of the letter of the law are hostile to the art of painting," wrote the court librarian. "The making of likenesses is a source of wisdom and an antidote against the poison of ignorance."

Akbar was a man of action and vision. In the administration of his empire he brought together Moslem and Hindu, encouraging the customs and practices of both. He married an Indian princess; and he received with honor Hindu priests and scholars as well as Portuguese merchants and Jesuit missionaries, who brought contact with the West.

Akbar's son, Jahangir, who ascended the throne in 1605, was observant and curious. A hunter, he became interested in living animals and banned hunting on

FIGHTING ELEPHANTS

certain days. His aviary contained four thousand singing birds. Among the animals in his menagerie were over a hundred lions; fifteen lion cubs had the freedom of his palace. "The flowers that are seen in the territories of Kashmir are beyond all calculation," he wrote in his memoirs. Emissaries to distant places were requested to bring home rare plants as well as animals and birds.

As a connoisseur of art he rivaled his father. He could identify an artist's work even if each head in a painting was by a different hand. Father Xavier, a Jesuit priest, describes the prince's delight in a collection of Western prints and drawings. The fusing of Persian, Indian, and Western elements in the art of his reign brought Mughal painting to its climax.

PAINTER AND SCRIBE

BLUE-THROATED BARBET, BY MANSUR

Records in Paint

Art under the Mughals was strictly controlled, refined, and costly. The painters were members of the royal household, receiving monthly salaries. The best paper and pigments were provided for their use. Precious lapis lazuli was ground to powder for the blues, cinnabar for reds, and ochre for yellows. Gold was used freely. Paintings were the work of the group. One artist would be responsible for design and layout, another for figures, another for color. The finished work was not signed, although sometimes the court clerk noted names in the margin. Many of the paintings under Akbar were illustrations for the great epic poems of Persia and India, which he loved. Perhaps because, strange to say, he had never learned to read, he demanded more and more pictorial records of the events of his reign.

Jahangir also favored pictures of events of his own times. "The old songs weary my heart," he said. "If we read at all, let it be what we have seen and beheld ourselves." Two or three painters accompanied the Emperor on all his travels. Names are mentioned: Manohar, Bichitr, Mansur. "Ustad Mansur has become the Wonder of the Age, and in the art of drawing is unique in his generation," said Jahangir in his memoirs, and added that Ustad Mansur had painted more than a hundred flowers. Mansur was famous also for his birds and animals. Jahangir speaks of a rare falcon that has come to his attention. "As it was something out of the common, I ordered Ustad Mansur to paint and preserve its likeness."

It was, perhaps, in the rendering of elephants that the Mughal painters showed their greatest skill. Always popular in Indian art, the huge creatures become marvels of energy with their poised bodies, sinuous trunks and crafty eyes. Their majesty dwarfs the spindly keepers who goad them to fight.

Portraits were painted for Jahangir of the high officials of his reign. Although the likenesses are accurately observed, an old tendency to show head and feet in profile and shoulders in a front view, is maintained. A flower in the hand indicates delight in women, a sword, military

A PRINCE RIDING AN ELEPHANT

ZEBRA, BY MANSUR

valor, and a hawk, prowess in the hunt.

In style Mughal painting brings together the sumptuous splendor and sure decorative sense of Persian art, the close observation and naturalism of the Indians, and European roundness and depth. Figures are modeled; landscape is rendered in perspective. European art of the seventeenth century was deeply concerned with the dramatic possibilities of light and shade. On the other hand, in Indian painting color and rich surface pattern were never marred by cast shadows.

"MICHELANGELO, SCULPTOR"

(1475–1564)

SELF-PORTRAIT AS JOSEPH OF ARIMATHEA

In a long lifetime of almost superhuman activity, Michelangelo showed himself to be the Renaissance ideal of a many-sided genius. Though talented as poet, expert as military engineer, brilliant as architect, superbly gifted as painter, he felt most at home in sculpture, signing even his paintings, "Michelangelo, Sculptor." He liked to claim that he had absorbed the love of stone and chisels from his nurse, the wife of a stonecutter in the quarries near Florence.

Though of noble birth, Michelangelo's parents were poor, and his formal education was brief. Showing extraordinary artistic talents, he was apprenticed at fourteen to Ghirlandajo, a panel and fresco painter, from whom he learned to draw and paint. It was at this time that Michelangelo's nose was crushed in a schoolboy fight, disfiguring him for life.

After a year with Ghirlandajo, Michelangelo was transferred to a sculpture academy in the gardens of Lorenzo de' Medici, ruler of Florence. Lorenzo, recognizing the boy's talent, invited him to live in the palace, where he had daily contact with the most brilliant philosophers and scholars of the time.

Lorenzo died in 1492 and Michelangelo, only seventeen, had to make his own way. He carved a *Cupid* so classical in style that it sold as an antique. The hoax was discovered, but admiration for the artist's skill led to his being invited to Rome where he received commissions from princes, cardinals and, in the course of his long life, from seven popes.

In 1505 Pope Julius II commissioned Michelangelo to prepare his tomb. Plans were drawn up and sketches presented, but the Pope changed his mind, postponed the tomb, and persuaded the sculptor to paint the ceiling of the Sistine Chapel. Four years later, this work finally finished, Michelangelo returned, with renewed enthusiasm, to the tomb; but Julius died in 1513 and the project was again pushed aside. In 1545, sadly reduced in size, it was finally completed. More

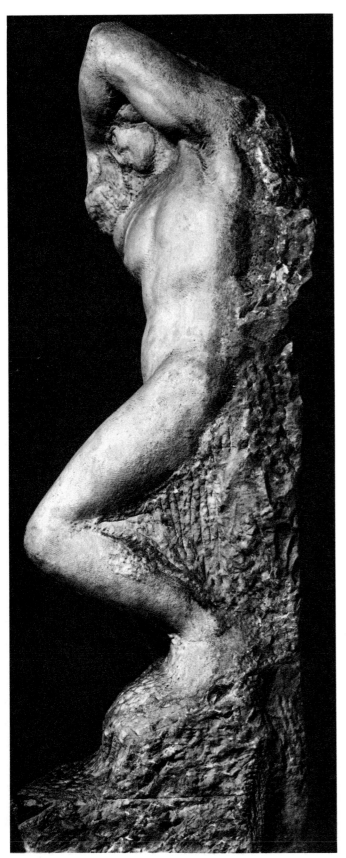

than forty figures were originally planned, but only seven appear, the most important being the powerful Moses, poised for action, yet, as a contemporary wrote, with a "face full of light and the Holy Spirit." His horns derive from a mistranslation of the Hebrew word used in the Bible for the light which suffused his face after God gave him the law on Mt. Sinai.

At seventy Michelangelo's energy and ability continued undiminished. Orders for paintings, sculpture, new buildings or the completion of old ones drove him from one commission to another. He was made architect of the Church of St. Peter which had long been under way in Rome. Although as it now stands it shows a number of later changes, the general scheme, and especially the enormous dome, are his work, another triumph in a long life of artistic achievement. He remained vigorous and worked to within a few days of his death at eighty-nine, his last sculpture as impressive as that of earlier years.

YOUNG SLAVE

DAVID

BEARDED SLAVE

Searching for Life Within Stone

Michelangelo saw in his mind's eye the figure within the stone block an conceived the act of carving as simply cutting away the unnecessary stone. After making preliminary drawings, and models in wax, he attacked the stone directly with hammer and chisel. He refused to consider as sculpture a work modele in clay. The early *Battle of Centaurs and Greeks* is in relief, the figures only partly freed from their background. They writhe and twist in their fight with each other almost as though struggling also against the stone that holds them down. The slaves, planned for the tomb of Pop

PIETÀ

OSES

BRUTUS

Julius II, and only half finished, give a similar impression. This sense of struggle is characteristic of much of Michelangelo's work.

Sketches for stones to be brought from the quarry show how surely he could estimate the mass necessary for each figure. When the Florentine government gave him a magnificent block of marble, some eighteen feet tall but narrow and already hacked by another sculptor, Michelangelo saw in it *David* preparing to attack Goliath, and fitted his design so exactly to the piece that the top of the head shows the roughness of the original block.

The master's early works show detail and high polish. The *Pietà* (Mary with the dead Christ in her arms), done during that first visit to Rome when the artist was in his early twenties, is quiet and profoundly moving, the only hint of agony being in the tortured drapery. This is Michelangelo's only signed work. Legend has it that he heard admirers attributing it to another artist and quietly chiseled his name on the band across Mary's chest.

Whether for lack of time or because he liked the play of imagination made possible by unfinished parts and surfaces, the later works were seldom completed. The roughed-in hair and ear, the tool marks on neck and face of the *Brutus* add to the sense of vigor and intensity in this ideal portrait of the patriot who destroys a tyrant. Drapery and pose were inspired by ancient coins and portrait busts, but the muscular neck, the alertness, and the expression of controlled anger seem to reflect Michelangelo's own bitter protest against oppression.

His last sculpture was another *Pietà* which he intended for his tomb. The Joseph of Arimathea, who looks down tenderly, has the features, it is said, of Michelangelo himself.

BATTLE OF CENTAURS AND GREEKS

Index of Artists, Pictures and Owners

Artists are listed alphabetically; the works are listed in the order in which they appear in the section devoted to each artist. Color plates are starred.

Photographic Credits

The author and publishers wish to thank all individuals and institutions who have made works of art in their possession available for reproduction.

Thanks is also due the following for photographs or prints reproduced on the pages mentioned:

Messrs. Alinari, Florence, 17 (right), 18 (bottom), 68, 112, 113, 114, 115, 116; © A.C.L., Brussels, 20; Oliver Baker Associates, New York, 40 (middle), 99, 111 (top); Henry B. Beville, Alexandria, Va., 10 (bottom), 37 (bottom); Joachim Blauel, Munich, 53 (bottom); J. E. Bulloz, Paris, 15 (bottom right); Conzett and Huber, Zurich, 40 (bottom), 100; Emiddio de Cusati, New Haven, Conn., 40 (top); John R. Freeman, London, 23, 46, 48 (bottom), 49, 53 (top), 65, 73 (bottom left and right), 102, 110, 111 (bottom); Giraudon, Paris, 16, 19, 26, 39, 42, 43, 52, 63, 69 (top), 75, 76, 79 (top and middle left), 95, 98 (top left), 104, 105; MAS, Barcelona, 32, 56, 57, 59 (bottom), 101, 103 (top, bottom middle); Francis G. Mayer, New York, 10 (top); Federico A. Mella, Milan, 69 (bottom); Erwin Meyer, Vienna, 61, 88, 89; Umberto Rossi, Venice, 17 (left), 18 (top); Charles E. Slatkin Galleries, New York, 38; George Spearman, London, 72 (right), 73 (top); Edward Steichen, 74; Walter Steinkopf, West Berlin, 92 (top left), 93 (bottom left); Taylor and Dull, New York, 25 (bottom).

DESIGNED BY ULRICH RUCHTI